D0078234

Tibetan Refugees

Margaret Nowak

Tibetan Refugees

Youth and the New Generation of Meaning

Rutgers University Press

New Brunswick, New Jersey

207585   305.8954
                N946

Library of Congress Cataloging in Publication Data

Nowak, Margaret, 1944–
  Tibetan refugees.

  Bibliography: p.
  Includes index.
  1. Tibetans—India.   2. Refugees, Political—India.
3. Refugees, Political—China—Tibet.   4. India—Social
life and customs.   I. Title.
DS432.T5N68 1983   305.8'954'054   82–22961
ISBN 0-8135-0979-3

Copyright © 1984 by Rutgers, The State University

All rights reserved

Manufactured in the United States of America

Just consider! Who are you? You say you've changed. In a week's time you may be yet another man. To whom do you expect to be loyal? To each one in turn? No, old man, it isn't like that. Loyalty is outside of us. You're forgetting that for many years you've been and still are one of us. That's what really matters. You're loyal to yourself if you're loyal to solidarity. That's what honour is, d'you see?

JERZY ANDRZEJEWSKI
Ashes and Diamonds

Contents

Acknowledgments

It would be impossible for me to acknowledge personally all those who have helped me bring to completion the creation of a book from the myriad experiences, thoughts, and reflections that have inspired it. The support and encouragement of my family, my professors-turned-into-colleagues, and my friends (the categories are by no means mutually exclusive) began long before I started the actual writing and has continued long after the formally designated research period gave way to a full-time university teaching career. Likewise, my fieldwork experience was replete with so much warm hospitality, generosity, and ever-ready assistance from both Tibetans and Indians that I cannot hope to do full justice to them all in this brief, formalized expression of my gratitude.

Despite the inherent limitations of such an endeavor, I would still like to mention certain key individuals whose contributions to my work have been especially significant: Mr. P. R. Mehendiratta and Mr. L. S. Suri of the American Institute of Indian Studies, New Delhi; Professor P. L. Mehra of Panjab University, Chandigarh; Rapten and Khando Chazotsang of the Tibetan Homes Foundations; and Dawa Norbu and Tsering Wangyal, past and present editors of *Tibetan Review*, respectively. Finally, I would like to express my special thanks to Jean-Paul Dumont, Lawrence Epstein, and Charles Ibsen for their sustained willingness to offer both personal encouragement and constructive criticism.

Introduction

'What is truth?' asked Pilate.
And even Christ did not (would not? could
not?) answer.
—A selectively remembered quotation:
from my own traditional past

When I tried to find these lines in an official source, I was disappointed. The New Testament passage in John (18:38) merely states, "'Truth?' said Pilate, 'What is that?'; and with that he went out again." Yet somehow this mistaken remembrance of mine and its theme for me—that truth cannot be grasped—may illuminate the real subject of this book more genuinely than the most lucid anthropological prose.

The people about whom this account is written, some of the 84,000 Tibetan refugees who have resettled in India since 1959, have also become in some ways distanced from their traditional past, though of course the reasons for and the intensity of, their severance from certainties formerly taken for granted are quite different from my own. Yet both they, as uprooted refugees, and I, their foreign anthropological-interpreter, have at least this much in common: in trying to understand our respective situations, we both have to deal with varying degrees of what the hermeneuticians would call "cultural estrangement." Furthermore, both they, striving to make sense of their tragic losses, subsequent disorientation, and now potentially open future, and I, the outsider attempting to interpret all this, must indeed confront, however consciously, the problem of truth and the possibility of apprehending it. What "is," what "is like," what "should be," such are the questions and reflections that affect and are affected by both of our attempts to understand despite the gaps and unfamiliarities, to rescue meaning from estrangement.

On the one hand, the Tibetan refugees of my 1976–1977 fieldwork experience have had to face a particular version of what Ricoeur (1976), in a slightly different context, has referred to as "distanciation."[1] For them, one of the most critical cultural (i.e., symbolic, nonbiological) problems to be confronted is that of continuing, adapting, or even losing their traditional cultural heritage. As Ricoeur (1976) has noted:

> A tradition raises no philosophical problem as long as we live and dwell within it in the naiveté of the first certainty. Tradition only becomes problematic when this first naiveté is lost. Then we have to retrieve its meaning through and beyond estrangement. Henceforth the appropriation of the past proceeds along an endless struggle with distanciation. Interpretation, philosophically understood, is nothing else than an attempt to make estrangement and distanciation productive. (p. 44)

Especially for the young generation educated in modern India, "the naiveté of the first certainty" has most definitely been lost, even for those who strenuously affirm themselves to be "traditional Tibetans." Yet despite the very real dangers that challenge their sense of personal and group integrity (alienation from self or other Tibetans, disillusionment over hopes and expectations that will never come true, confused ethnic identity in the wake of the Tibetan diaspora), these people are indeed struggling to interpret their situation; that is, they are attempting to rescue the possibility of an ongoing cultural heritage by elaborating, refashioning, and creating new meaning out of the dialectical interaction of their past and present ideologies and experience.

On the other hand, my own situation as foreign anthropologist-interpreter was also marked by some measure of distanciation and estrangement. Most obviously I was an alien, an "other" who shared neither the Tibetans' historical, social, and personal backgrounds nor, more fundamentally, the full range of their traditional assumptions about the nature of reality. Yet any honest reflection on this state of affairs presented me with a paradoxical insight. When I stopped thinking about "the Tibetans" and thought instead about my closest friends and confidants, Pema, Tsewang, Rigzin, and Tashi,

---

1. The main point of Ricoeur's discussion concerns the hermeneutic problem of interpreting written historical texts from a past era, especially in cases where the culture involved has undergone great change since the time of the writing. Elsewhere, however, Ricoeur (1971, 1981) does specifically acknowledge the applicability of his ideas to "anthropology and the other social sciences" (1976: 861).

there were times when I felt far more alienated from certain aspects, institutions, assumptions, and even individuals of my own culture. The whole enterprise of doing fieldwork and completing a dissertation, for example, troubled me more than once precisely because distanciation and estrangement seemed so essential to the process. At the most apparent level, of course, I, like every anthropologist, had to contend with the need for some degree of objective detachment vis-à-vis these people who were the source of my data. On further reflection, however, I noted a more problematic kind of estrangement: I too had lost "the naiveté of the first certainty" with respect to my tradition, and nowhere did my tradition impinge so significantly on my anthropologizing as it did on the issue of "truth."

I had already encountered the problem of multiple ontologies and epistemologies via previous courses in Buddhist and Western philosophy, but those encounters could always be bracketed off from my life, where my whole social world said "of course" and "of course not" with hardly a thought about the finite limitations of all world views, our own included. As open as I might try to be to the implications of that cardinal virtue of anthropology, cultural relativity, I could scarcely claim to have been unaffected by Enlightenment assumptions about rationality and truth and about the priority of my tradition's ontological world and epistemological criteria. Stated simply, others' interpretations may indeed be acknowledged as profound or poetic, but in the end, it is ours that are unquestioningly assumed to yield primary access to the real truths of existence.

During the time of my fieldwork and dissertation writing, reflections such as these only came to the surface in embryonic form; I saw at that time a much greater need to finish my work than to philosophize. Subsequently, however, I discovered that such ideas have been at the core of full-blown investigations in the field of philosophical hermeneutics, particularly as elaborated by Gadamer (1975/ 1960, 1976). Central to Gadamer's concern is his notion of "understanding" as "a fusion of horizons," a paradigm I find most instructive in its applicability to cross-cultural, philosophically grounded research. What has evolved from my dissertation, then, is really a study within a study: an interpretation of the changing horizon, or outlook of possibilities, of contemporary Tibetan refugees, set within a broader consideration of the horizon of the interpretation itself, mine and that of my disciplinary tradition in particular.

The central focus of this book is very definitely on the Tibetan refugees and their attempts to affect and be affected by some of their key symbols. My wider concern here—the implications of trying to *understand*, both anthropologically and philosophically—is a much more recent subject of my research and reflection; thus the seams binding the two levels of investigation may at times be visible, especially to readers expecting a finished statement on these matters. Nevertheless, even at this preliminary stage I can positively identify a central theme integrating both levels of consideration: the issue of tradition.

In my dissertation (Nowak, 1978b) I examined the traditional symbol of the Dalai Lama in relation to the newly developing metaphor of *rangzen* (literally, "self power"; conventionally translated as "independence" in the obvious political sense and suggestive of a broad range of metapolitical life strategies for these people).[2] In considering this particular interplay between past and present, ideology and experience, I have adapted Turner's (1967) concept of "liminality," extending it to apply to the special case of stateless refugee exile and focusing in particular on the notion of ambiguity in his general thesis (i.e., that symbols and metaphors proliferate in the ambiguity of liminal states) as a means of explaining socially based symbolic innovation in this particular cultural context. In this connection, the critical issue of tradition might best be elucidated in reference to the transmission of both old (the Dalai Lama) and the newly emerging (*rangzen*) symbolic complexes; thus my Tibetan data is roughly organized into two parts, the first dealing with deliberate, more or less primary socialization, the second, with the later learning that occurs as a result of the confrontation between carefully presented ideologies and actual social experience.

I have broadened the scope of my previous research, going beyond considerations of symbolic anthropology to engage in some speculation about the wider problem of interpretation.in general. Here the

---

2. For those who are not Tibetan specialists, Tibetan orthography, with its "silent" letters and "unpredictable" consonant clusters, can present a formidable problem. The actual Tibetan spelling, transliterated according to the system I use throughout this book (see Wylie, 1959), is *rang-btsan*; however, the term is commonly anglicized as *rangzen* by Tibetans familiar with English. Both forms appear in this book, depending on whether my emphasis is on the idea of independence or on the literal meaning of the Tibetan morphemes.

issue of tradition and its transmission, particularly that of my world-view and discipline, demands a more reflective treatment than the Tibetan material. In this connection, then, the ideas of Gadamer and Ricoeur have been most instructive for me. Following their lead, my intent here is to explore some of the implications of the insight that understanding, mediated by all the prejudgments and partially answered questions that precede and accompany it, involves opening up one's own ontological world. In this way, this book represents an attempt to increase Western self-knowledge as well as Western knowledge of contemporary Tibetan refugees, for in different ways both they and members of our culture face a similar problem: overcoming the gap between past or alien tradition, and present but not yet perfected attempts at meaningful interpretation.

Chapter One

Interpreting Tibetan Refugees in India

Distanciation is most definitely a fact of life for the vast majority of Tibetan refugees, who feel estranged from both their past identity (however idealized) as secure citizens of their own nation-state and from their present circumstances as alien residents of a foreign host country. A less extreme yet generally parallel statement could likewise be made concerning my own situation as anthropologist-interpreter in India. What is common in both instances is the newcomer's perceptions of severed connections and multiple images of reality, the "back-and-forth reflections and refractions" of what one is or believes oneself to be and what society says one is or ought to be (Read, 1980: 96).

In his study of the "style" or "lore" of a male homosexual tavern, Read (1980) explores the latter theme masterfully, particularly in relation to a phrase he has borrowed from theater-of-the-absurd literature: the "hall of mirrors." In the context of my study, I emphasize a slightly different interpretation of this phrase; whereas Read equates "hall of mirrors" with "hall of culture" (ultimately invoking the metaphor of society as prison), I focus less on the negative connotations of cultural imprisonment and more on the idea of a hall of mirrors as a virtually infinite progression of images. I look at myself trying to make sense of the situation of young Tibetans in India and see reflection after reflection of both of our attempts to rescue meaning.

The parallels between their situation and mine (both of us seeking meaningful interpretation) are hardly perfect, for the very word *Tibetans* is, of course, a reification in a way that the pronoun *I* is not. Nevertheless, when this and all other qualifications are acknowledged, it is still the case that both they and I shared certain problems and strategies in our quest to make sense of it all. First, for various reasons and to varying degrees, we had both lost "the naiveté of the first certainty." In other words, not only had their tradition as Tibetans been rendered problematic by the course of events, but my self-definition vis-à-vis my various social roles—American, single woman, graduate student in anthropology, and so on—was likewise challenged by my sudden immersion in Tibetan refugee society, in turn set within modern Indian society.

Related to this is the fact that both they and I were being doubly socialized by our situations: they, by Tibetan institutions-in-exile, which were deliberately promulgating traditional ideologies as much as possible, yet also by the pragmatic lessons of actual social experience in their new environment; myself, by a similar ideal/real dichotomy of expectations stemming from formal graduate school training versus actual fieldwork.

Finally, both they and I had to deal constantly with multiple levels of ambiguity.[1] Theirs, I explore in detail later in this book; regarding my own situation, I was and yet was not "clearly American"; I was and yet was not "a woman living alone in India"; I was and yet was not "an anthropologist primarily engaged in field research." Despite the apparently obvious implications of my passport, sex, and research paraphernalia (notebooks, camera, and other such props), not one of these aspects of my self-definition—nationality, gender, or profession—was completely unambiguous in my own or anyone else's eyes. Of course I was American most of the time, but then again, in conversations with Tibetans about ethnic versus mainstream-society affiliation, I could also define myself as "Polish-American-who-grew-up-in-a-Polish neighborhood." Similarly, I was without question a woman alone in India as I traveled on buses or shopped in bazaars by myself. Yet by speaking Tibetan to any Tibetans nearby, even total strangers, I could confound some of the assumptions and expectations that natives were likely to have, given

1. For a superb treatment of this sort of ambiguity, see Kaminski (1980). Kaminski began his study of Polish gypsies first in Poland, where and when he was a citizen of that country; then he did fieldwork in Czechoslovakia, where, as a foreigner, he was regarded with suspicion by the local authorities. By the time he was studying Polish gypsies at his third research site, Sweden, his own status had changed from Polish citizen to immigrant researcher to refugee himself, at which point his theoretical focus on strategies of "passing" and ethnic signaling had direct implications for his own situation as well.

what they initially thought they saw: an unaccompanied "European" woman. I could also manipulate local stereotypes about being "only a woman" to my advantage, slipping in and out of sensitive situations (to take a picture, get an interview, etc.) without being perceived as highly visible or threatening.

Finally, my official definition as "anthropologist-doing-doctoral-research" likewise applied to only one aspect of my identity there. While in India collecting material for my dissertation, my personal life went on as unremittingly as ever: a death in my family at home, changes in several important relationships, deeply affecting impressions (scenes and scenery witnessed, journal entries pondered, books read, even dreams at night), and a few very close friendships with people who happened to be Tibetan. Such experiences prompted me more than once to look very critically at my otherwise necessary role playing and acknowledge, in Goffmanesque fashion, the various levels of impression management required by my fieldwork and doctoral-candidate situation.

My aim in reflecting on these ideas, however, is not disclosure as an end in itself. Rather, I see the hall-of-mirrors analogy as extremely relevant here. By considering the "back-and-forth reflections and refractions" of what Tibetan refugees are and I am (or what we believe ourselves to be) and what our respective cultural traditions say we are or ought to be, I believe both of our attempts to rescue meaning can be illuminated, in respect not only to specific images in the mirror but ultimately to the critical issue of ontologies and epistemologies.

In progressing toward this final goal of the present work—examining the implications of trying to understand the other—I pay much more attention to the ethnographic case at hand than to my personal biography. Thus this book is essentially devoted to an exposition of Tibetans' situation as refugees, with much less explicit consideration given to analyzing my situation as anthropologist-interpreter. Nevertheless it is important to recognize the commonalities in both sets of circumstances: both they and I often used a similar strategy of playing off various ambiguities in our lives, one against the other. For both of us, the hall of mirrors provided cracks to slip through as well as images of what is and what ought to be. In this sense, then, the is/ought dialectic may be seen as the leitmotif that appears again and again throughout this book, variously conceptualized as the relationship between real and ideal, experience and ideology, present and past, or familiar and alien.

Historical Background

The focus of this work, then, is the Tibetan refugees, specifically the young generation, who have left Tibet and have resettled (or were born) in India after the abortive anti-Chinese uprising and the Dalai Lama's flight to political asylum in that country in March 1959. I am thus dealing with only a small proportion of the total Tibetan population, which has been estimated to have been between 2 and 3 million in the years just before the Chinese occupation.[2] Of this number, approximately 100,000 have successfully fled Tibet to begin new lives elsewhere.[3] According to the Office of Tibet in New York City (personal communication, August 10, 1982), 86,000 Tibetans now live in India; 10,000 in Nepal; 2,000 in Bhutan; 1,000 in Switzerland; 500 elsewhere in Europe (mainly in Scandinavia, Germany, France, Holland, and Great Britain); 500 in Canada; and 250 in the United States.

Since 1959–1961, the peak years of exodus immediately following the flight of the Dalai Lama and his cabinet, the number of Tibetans still escaping has dropped considerably. It would appear that the

2. This figure is from Richardson (1962: 6), who served as a British diplomat in Tibet from 1936 to 1940, in 1944, and from 1946 to 1950. The Tibetan press in India speaks, however, of 6 million left behind, a number that includes the region of Khams and Amdo (see *Tibetan Review*, 1976k: 5). Actually, the problem of varying population statistics is an old one, compounded by the necessity of distinguishing between "three Tibets" (Karan, 1976: 5): "cultural Tibet" (including all areas at one time inhabited exclusively or predominantly by people of Tibetan extraction); "geographical Tibet" (including parts of Sinkiang and Sikang, i.e., Khams and Amdo); and "political Tibet" (including only that part of geographical and cultural Tibet ruled by the Tibetan government from earliest times to 1951). As Mehra (1968) points out, "In 1907 the Chinese government computed the population at 6,430,000, while 15 years later its figure fell to 1,500,000! This leaves a margin of five million between the lowest and the highest estimates, which obviously vary according to the physical boundaries one keeps in view" (p. 22). This same kind of numbers game can be noted in an article in *Tibetan Review* (1978c) which compares the figures released by Peking in May of that year (1,630,000 ethnic Tibetans) with the Dharamsala-held figure of "between six to seven million as the population of Tibet before 1959" (p. 4).

3. Actually, 100,000 represents a rather conservative estimate of the number of Tibetans who have tried to escape, for many hundreds if not thousands have died in unsuccessful attempts to cross the Himalayas on foot.

sharp decline in refugee attempts is due primarily to increasing border surveillance by the Chinese, who are supported in their efforts by Nepalese border guards; there is definitely no indication that Tibetans in Tibet are coming to accept Chinese rule. In fact, despite some reports to the contrary by recent Western visitors to Tibet, who are overwhelmingly dependent on Chinese interpreters and staged tours for their impressions of "Tibet today,"—the young Tibetan generation appears to be persisting in their parents' attitudes, with this ironic addition: they are criticizing what they see as Chinese colonialism on the basis of "authentic" community theory.[4]

A further problem with statistics on refugee numbers arises from the fact that Tibetan agencies such as the Tibet Office in New York City make no distinction between those Tibetans who have actually fled Tibet and those who have been born in exile. From the Tibetans' own perspective, both groups are refugees. Especially in India, the vast majority of Tibetans prefer to define themselves legally as noncitizens of their host country, willingly (though not always happily) subjecting themselves to the resulting sociopolitical ambiguity of being stateless. In this way, they are attempting to preserve their sense of loyalty to Tibet, their home country, and to keep alive the dream of someday being able to return to their homeland, with the proviso that it still be a Buddhist nation under the supreme leadership of the Dalai Lama.

As for the social backgrounds of these refugees, again, there are simply no exact and unambiguous demographic statistics available. While in India, my own impression was that approximately 90 percent of the families I met there were commoners rather than traditional nobility; in other words, probably only about 10 percent of these families were *sger-pa*, or enfeoffed with an inheritable patrimonial estate. When the first groups of Tibetans began emigrating to the West, however, it was the former aristocrats who predominated numerically. Today their number is declining because of the pattern of family emigrations following the arranged marriage between India-reared young people (usually daughters) and compatibly aged Tibetans already established in such countries as Switzerland, Canada, and the United States.

4. For documentation, see *Tibet under Chinese Rule* (1976) and the regular monthly feature of *Tibetan Review* entitled "Tibet News."

Tibetan explanations for the diaspora typically mention fear of persecution as a key motivating factor. For those that fled, the decision followed upon a personal conviction that life in Tibet had become unendurable. I present the following account of a 42-year-old farmer from southern Tibet so that one of these refugees may speak for himself. The volume from which it comes, *Tibet under Chinese Communist Rule* (1976), was compiled by Tibetans associated with the Dalai Lama's government-in-exile in Dharamsala, the Tibetans' de facto capital-in-exile. They have translated the statements into English and edited them slightly by omitting their concluding lines (an oath as to their truthfulness and accuracy) and by deleting "unqualified personal interpretations of events and actions, expressions of hopes and prayers, and emotional descriptions of the Chinese" (p. v). In the farmer's statement, I have altered the order of four sentences in order to avoid quoting an excessively long passage.

> We [the narrator, his wife, and daughter] escaped from Tibet because life was getting more and more difficult, and tension and fear of persecution was increasing every year. We had nothing that we could call our own. Everything belonged to the commune or the Chinese. . . . The Chinese demand labour from the people and take away most of the products from the lands for themselves. The people are, in fact, slaves of an alien conqueror. The amount of food available is barely enough to feed half the population. Heavy taxes are levied on every article of daily need. . . . What was most unbearable was the increasing hardship and mental torture.
>
> I was classified as a middle-class peasant and continually harassed for the "crimes" I had never committed. Last year, I decided to escape. The Chinese somehow came to know of it. I was blacklisted and accused of "turning away from the proletarian socialist revolutionary path and following the way of reactionary Dalai bandits." I was given the alternative of either making a frank confession of my crimes and wrong thoughts or else facing public trials, imprisonment and torture. I could not change my thoughts as the Chinese wanted, and knew that the only change I was going to bring to the whole situation was escaping from Tibet. On the night of March 2, 1971, while everybody was attending the nightly study-cum-meeting ses-

sion, we fled and headed towards the Nepalese border.
(pp. 126–127)

Examples such as this, multiplied by the thousands, can of course serve as individual explanations for the Tibetan diaspora, but the historical and political antecedents of this situation still remain to be clarified. It should be immediately pointed out, however, that the issues involved here are part of an exceedingly tangled web of centuries of policies, politics, precedents, and legal ambiguities; and it is not my intent here to proclaim any final untangling of these matters. What follows, then, is only a very simplified outline of Sino-Tibetan contact and relations leading up to the mass exodus that began in 1959.

Whereas Tibetans themselves consider their existence as a unified nation to have begun with the reign of Gnya'-khri btsan-po (correlated with the year 127 B.C. in *Tibetan Review*, 1973b: 10), Western scholars usually use the great Tibetan king Srong-btsan sgam-po (r. A.D. 627–650) to mark the commencement of safely datable Tibetan history. From the seventh to the ninth centuries, Tibet's policy was one of aggressive military campaigns and territorial expansion. For a brief 15-day period in 763, the army even succeeded in placing a Tibetan emperor on the Chinese throne at Ch'ang-an (present-day Sian) after having invaded this southern capital. At intervals during these centuries of warfare and conquest, Tibet's political authority extended past Afghanistan as far as Samarkand in the west, deep into Chinese Turkestan and China itself in the north and east, and through Nepal and into northern India and northern Burma in the south (Richardson, 1962: 2). The westward expansion of the Tibetan army between the years 785 and 805 caused the Arabian caliph of Baghdad, Harun al-Rashid, to join forces with the Chinese in order to curb the power of these all-too-successful Central Asian warriors (Shakabpa, 1967: 44). In view of the contrast between those early days of blood and thunder and today's mood of national shame and self-doubt, it is hardly coincidental that a quotation about this event by the Italian Tibetologist Petech (1939) has become a current favorite in the Tibetan press (it has appeared in *Tibetan Review* and is also cited by the Tibetan author Shakabpa): "The very fact that nothing less than the coalition of the two most powerful empires of the early Middle Ages was necessary for checking the expansion of the Tibetan states, is a magnificent witness of the political capacities and military valour of those sturdy mountaineers" (pp. 73–74).

The end of Tibet's domination over Central Asia came in 842 with the assassination of the king Glang-dar-ma by a monk, Lha-lung Dpal-gyi rdo-rje, who had decided to put an end in this way to the sovereign's anti-Buddhist persecutions. (The theme of violence justified by a higher religious goal is thus an old one in Tibetan historical consciousness.) For the next four centuries there was no centralized political rule in Tibet; authority fragmented into numerous small hegemonies, whose warring and intriguing rulers gradually allied themselves with one or the other of the major Buddhist monastic orders of that time: Sakya (*sa-skya*), Kagyupa (*bka'-rgyud-pa*), or the latter's subsect, Karmapa (*kar-ma-pa*).

By the early part of the thirteenth century, it was the Mongols who were fast becoming the dominant power of north and central Asia. They had already subjugated the Tangut (Hsi-hsia) empire (present-day Kansu and Ch'ing-hai provinces) and were on their way to the total conquest of China itself. Fearing the devastation of their lands and monasteries, the leading nobles and abbots of Tibet sent a delegation to Genghis Khan with an offer of submission. The offer was accepted, and Tibet was able to preserve her autonomy by surrendering, though as it turned out, only nominally, to a foreign suzerain.

This historical event, followed by a chain of others, eventually culminated in "that peculiar relationship between Tibet and China known as *yon-mchod*, "Patron and Priest," by which the ruler of Tibet in the person of the predominant grand lama was regarded as the religious advisor and priest of the Emperor, who in return acted as patron and protector" (Snellgrove and Richardson, 1968: 148). As further explained by a Tibetan who himself served in the Tibetan government up to 1951:

> This relationship . . . cannot be defined in Western political terms. . . . It was maintained as the basis of a political relationship between the Tibetans and the Mongols; and in later times, between the Manchu Emperor and the Dalai Lama. The patron–lama relationship with the Manchus ended in 1911, with the overthrow of the Ch'ing Dynasty. (Shakabpa, 1967: 71)

Without an adequate understanding of the *yon-mchod* relationship, the fundamental disaccord today between Tibet and China (both mainland and Taiwan) cannot be properly comprehended. For this reason, I present here a very basic summary of the evolution of this institution, keeping in mind my ultimate aim in this historical discussion: elucidating significant themes in Tibetan historical consciousness (e.g., the military glory of the early kings; the precedent of violence—regicide—justified by a noble, i.e., religion-affirming, purpose; and now, the development of a polity that would combine sacred and temporal political power in one quintessentially symbolic figure). In addition, my examination of the priest–patron relationship must encompass two related observations: first, this institution was operative during dynastic periods when the emperor on the Chinese throne was not, in fact Han (ethnic Chinese); second, in reference to Sino-Tibetan contact and relations at other times, the situation was such that "Chinese political theory excluded entirely the possibility of equal diplomatic relations with any other country whatsoever" (Snellgrove and Richardson, 1968: 198).

The *yon-mchod* relationship between Tibetan lama[5] and imperial patron began to take shape in 1244 when the grandson of Genghis Khan, Prince Godan, invited the head lama of the Sakya monastery to serve as religious preceptor for himself and his people. Sixteen years later the prince's son, Kublai Khan, soon to become emperor of China, received religious consecration from the Sakya lama's monk nephew, 'phags-pa blo-gros rgyal-mtshan. In return, the Mongol ruler gave the lama the title *ti-shih* (帝師 , "imperial preceptor") and invested the office with spiritual and temporal authority over Dbus-gtsang (central Tibet), Khams, and Amdo. In 1279 the Mongols' conquest of China was complete; from that time until the last years of the Yüan dynasty, the emperors of China conducted their relations with Tibet through the *ti-shih*—an office always held by a lama (Richardson, 1962: 34).

In the final decade before the fall of the Yüan and the reestablish-

---

5. Despite the no longer rare occurrence of this term in Western publications, its authentic Tibetan meaning can be problematic. As M. Goldstein (1968: 165n) points out, the word *lama* (*bla-ma*; literally, "superior one") "is a difficult term to translate in English. It refers to a renowned religious personage who usually, although not necessarily, was also an incarnation. Lama may also refer to the person who has faith in or the person one received religious teaching from."

ment of a native Chinese dynasty (Ming, 1368–1644), Tibet witnessed the beginnings of a nationalistic revival on its own soil, with the glorification of the early kings as one of its prominent themes. Factions and rivalries allied and opposed noble families and great monasteries, and there was no single leader, religious or lay, who enjoyed universal support. During this period, the new Chinese rulers adopted the Mongols' policy of bestowing honorary ranks on various heads of religious orders, but in this case it was lay princes, and not lamas, who were the governing leaders of Tibet. Over these lay rulers, "the Ming dynasty exercised neither authority nor influence" (Richardson, 1962: 36, 38).

Also at this time, an important new Tibetan Buddhist sect was founded: the Gelugpa (*dge-lugs-pa*). With its strong emphasis on learning and strict monastic discipline, this order, right from the start, had the makings of an effective bureaucracy (Snellgrove and Richardson, 1968: 228). This administrative potential was in fact soon utilized, and the Gelugpas came to predominate in both front- and backstage workings of that uniquely Tibetan religious-political system: the institution of the Dalai Lama.

Long before the inauguration of this supreme Tibetan office, the idea of metempsychosis was already an integral part of popular Buddhist belief; nevertheless, the manipulation of this theory for the purpose of directing successorship or otherwise identifying a continuous lineage of religious power holders only came about with the development of religiously based interest groups who could, in this way, gain prestige by thus affirming their link with a great figure of the past. When the founder of the Gelugpa order died, his successor was found in his close disciple and nephew, Dge-'dun grub-pa (1391–1475), "an unusually clever man . . . [who] at the same time . . . was an intriguer . . . who did everything possible to consolidate the hierarchical system of the Yellow Church [Gelugpa order]" (Hoffman, 1961: 168). A few years after the death of this figure, it was recognized that a young monk, Dge-'dun rgya-mtsho (1475–1542), was in fact Dge-'dun grub-pa's reincarnation; preparatory prophecies had been made known during the first hierarch's lifetime, and the acknowledged reincarnation had, in fact, been born shortly after the death of the former.

In a similar fashion, the reincarnation of Dge-'dun rgya-mtsho was found in a child, Bsod-nams rgya-mtsho (1543–1588), who was to become a brilliant scholar and a zealous missionary. It was this monastic hierarch who was the first to be recognized in his own lifetime as "Dalai Lama"; the title was bestowed on him by a powerful Mongol prince whom he converted in the course of his proselytizing activities in Mongolia. (The word *dalai* in Mongolian translates the Tibetan *rgya-mtsho*, "ocean," and presumably refers honorifically to the title bearer's "ocean of wisdom.") As Bsod-nams rgya-mtsho was already the third in a series of previously recognized reincarnations, the title was applied posthumously to his two predecessors, making him in fact the third Dalai Lama.

Despite this recognition, however, neither the third Dalai Lama nor his successor, Yon-tan rgya-mtsho (1589–1616), was considered the supreme regious-political ruler of Tibet. This period of Tibetan history saw the central region of the country torn apart by fierce fighting between the ruling princes of Dbus province, allied with the Gelugpa sect, and the king of Gtsang, supported by the Karmapa. Foreign intervention again played a major role in the outcome of events: the fourth Dalai Lama was a Mongol (a great-grandson of the prince who had given the title to Bsod-nams rgya-mtsho), and the Gelugpas thus relied on and received Mongolian support in their fight against the Gtsang nobility and the Karmapa.

In this atmosphere of religious and secular factions and alliances, it was the fifth Dalai Lama, Ngag-dbang blo-bzang rgya-mtsho (1617–1682), who became "the first Tibetan ruler who effectively united in his person both the spiritual and the temporal power" (Snellgrove and Richardson, 1968: 200). This occurred in 1642 when a powerful Mongol leader, Gushri Khan, defeated the king of Gtsang and "conferred on the Dalai Lama supreme authority over all Tibet from Tachienlu in the east up to the Ladakh border in the west: (Shakabpa, 1967: 111). The gesture of course recalls the Mongolian-Tibetan patron–lama relationship of four centuries past, but with these important differences: the Mongols were no longer emperors of China; the enthroned lama was now in his home country rather than at the imperial court; and finally, "the long process of adjustment between the Buddhist hierarchy and the lay nobility" had at last culminated in a unique type of government in which the Dalai Lama would be considered the supreme spiritual and temporal leader of Tibet (Richardson, 1962: 38).

The three centuries that separate us today from the founding of

Ganden Phodrang (*dga'-ldan pho-brang*, the system of Tibetan government described above) are well described by Richardson (1962), and Shakabpa (1967), Petech (1950), and Mehra (1968) among others; here I only point out that the period surrounding and immediately following the reign of the "Great Fifth" (as the fifth Dalai Lama is known by Tibetans) coincided with the fall of the Ming dynasty in China; the rise of Manchu power; the elaboration of the office of regent (*sde-srid*, the Dalai Lama's chief political administrator and de facto ruler during the time of the latter's minority); further wars and intrigues with foreign neighbors; and very significantly, the beginnings of the Chinese (Manchu) protectorate in Tibet.

As for the succession of Dalai Lamas who followed the "Great Fifth," their names and dates follow below;[6] what is important to notice is the enormous potential such an institution holds for being manipulated by private interest groups, for the recurrent gaps of time when the Dalai Lama was not old enough or did not live long enough to rule certainly did not discourage political scheming around the office of the regent.

Dalai Lama	Lived	Ruled
Sixth, Tshangs-dbyangs rgya-mtsho[7]	1683–1706	
Seventh, Bskal-bzang rgya-mtsho	1708–1757	1751–1757
Eighth, 'Jam-dpal rgya-mtsho	1758–1804	1781–1804
Ninth, Lung-rtogs rgya-mtsho	1806–1815	
Tenth, Tshul-khrims rgya-mtsho	1816–1837	
Eleventh, Mkhas-'grub rgya-mtsho	1838–1856	
Twelfth, 'Phrin-las rgya-mtsho	1856–1875	1873–1875
Thirteenth, Thub-bstan rgya-mtsho	1876–1933	1895–1933
Fourteenth, Bstan-'dzin rgya-mtsho	1935–	1950–

6. Names and dates of birth and death are from Shakabpa (1967: 346–347); dates of reign, when applicable, from M. Goldstein (1968: 165–166). Goldstein also notes that from 1751 to 1950, "there was a shift in ruler on the average of every 13 years, with Regents ruling 77 per cent of the time. If we exclude the reign of the 13th Dalai Lama (1895–1933), we see that Regents ruled approximately 94 per cent of the time" (p. 166).

7. The sixth Dalai Lama was an unusual figure for this office: a man-about-town who wrote poignant lyrical poetry, enjoyed the company of Lhasa courtesans, and very readily renounced his monastic vows. His unlikely behavior (for Dalai Lama, at least) can very possibly be explained by his lack of early childhood socialization for this role: the regent of the previous Dalai Lama (said to be the natural son of the "Great Fifth") had concealed the latter's death for 12 years while effectively and capably rul-

To resume the historical summary of this institution, then, let me briefly reconsider the point I had reached in this diachronic overview. The death of the fifth Dalai Lama in 1682 was followed by a series of wars and intrigues that culminated in Chinese involvement in Tibetan affairs. Nevertheless, during the period of the Manchu protectorate (1720–1911), the government still remained in Tibetan hands; furthermore, by the nineteenth century, China's "patron" role as military advisor and protector had become limited to the presence of two Manchu *ambans* (imperial representatives) and a small garrison in Lhasa. When the Manchu empire collapsed in 1911, Tibet formally declared its independence—"on the reasonable grounds that in the absence of an Emperor, their relationships with the Manchu house were at an end" (Denwood, 1975: 14[8]). By the end of the next year, the Tibetans had deported all Chinese residents, including the *ambans* and the garrison.

> This left something of a military vacuum in . . . [Tibet], which the Chinese themselves were incapable of filling consistently until after the communist takeover in 1949—though naturally they tried, by a combination of diplomacy and, where feasible, military efforts to retain as much influence as possible.
> . . . Stabilisation was sought through a tripartite conference of the major interested powers—the Simla Conference on Tibet between Tibet, Britain and China of 1913–1914. (Denwood, 1975: 14)

The two Asian parties came to this meeting with claims and counterclaims regarding the legality of Tibet's status as an independent state.

---

ing himself during that period. In any case, attempts by non-Tibetan authorities to depose the sixth Dalai Lama and replace him with another were never accepted by the Tibetan people, who continued to regard Tshangs-dbyangs rgya-mtsho as the only legitimate incarnation of the fifth, and the authentic predecessor of the seventh, Dalai Lama. The present Dalai Lama's elder brother devotes a whole chapter of one of his books to explaining Tibetan people's love and regard for this man and his poetry. See "A Riddle of Love" (Thubten Jigme Norbu and Turnbull, 1970: 279–293).

8. This article, which compares the fates of Mongolia and Tibet in the twentieth century, is the result of a seminar held at the London School of Oriental and African Studies. Other participants included C. R. Bawden, H. E. Richardson, and D. L. Snellgrove.

In an attempt to resolve the irreconcilable stands taken by the Chinese and Tibetan representatives, Sir Henry McMahon, on February 17, 1914, proposed a division of the disputed area into Inner and Outer Tibet, with Chinese suzerainty over Tibet. The Tibetans were unwilling to accept any form of Chinese overlordship in Tibet, and the Chinese were unwilling to accept the proposed boundaries; but for the sake of settling the dispute, the Tibetans reluctantly agreed to McMahon's proposal.

Under the terms of the proposed convention, Britain and China would recognize that Tibet was under the suzerainty of China. China would recognize the autonomy of Outer Tibet and would agree to abstain from interfering in the administration of that area, as well as in the selection and installation of the Dalai Lama. China was not to convert Tibet into a Chinese province, and Britain was to make no annexations. The Chinese would not send troops into Outer Tibet or attempt to station officials or establish colonies there. All Chinese troops and officials still in Tibet had to be withdrawn within three months of the signing of the Convention. The Chinese would be permitted to send a high official, with an escort not to exceed three hundred men, to reside in Lhasa. (Shakabpa, 1967: 254)

The draft of this document was merely initialed by the Chinese representative, and the Chinese government ultimately instructed him not to sign the final copy. After more than four months of delays and Chinese counterproposals, the British representative sent a communiqué to the Chinese, stating that "unless the Convention is signed before the end of the month, His Majesty's Government will hold themselves free to sign separately with Tibet" (Shakabpa, 1967: 255). That, in fact, is exactly what happened:

The Chinese Government never ratified the Simla Convention, preferring to retain their option of conquering Tibet at some future time. Contacts between Britain and Tibet thus took place without reference to the Chinese, who continued to make various overtures to the Tibetan government. . . . The Chinese Nationalist government was never seriously in

a position to invade Tibet, which acted throughout the period
as an independent state, although the Nationalists never gave
up their claim that Tibet was part of China. It was only in
1950 that the Chinese communist army forced the Tibetan
government into a reluctant cooperation with China—cooperation which enabled the Chinese to entrench themselves sufficiently to suppress the uprising in 1959 and take complete control of
Tibet. (Denwood, 1975: 15)

This summary of events leading up to the uprising in 1959 is, of
course, greatly abridged, and for similar reasons of economy, I conclude with only a brief outline of the Lhasa revolt. Historical works
cited earlier, particularly those by Richardson and Shakabpa, cover
the period immediately preceding 1959 quite thoroughly, as does the
Dalai Lama in his autobiography (Dalai Lama XIV, 1962). In addition, an insider's view of eastern (Khams and Amdo) Tibetan resistance to the Chinese between 1950 and 1959 is provided by the
Khampa guerilla leader Andrugtsang (1973).

The twentieth-century buildup of Chinese strength in Tibet began
late in 1949 with large-scale troop movements in the vicinity of
Chamdo, the regional capital of eastern Tibet located about 400
miles northeast of Lhasa. The (Chinese) People's Liberation Army,
claiming as its goal "the liberation of Tibet from foreign imperial-
ists," captured Chamdo in October of that year. Following this invasion, the Tibetan National Assembly appealed to the United Nations
for assistance, but the question was never taken up because of lack
of support from Britain and India. The Dalai Lama, then 15 years of
age, had been hastily invested with full power as ruler of Tibet; with
Chinese presence in Lhasa an imminent certainty, he had but three
courses open to him:

> flight across the southern border into India, diehard last-ditch
> resistance in Lhasa, or a deal with the communist invaders.
> Since it was now clear that no power on earth was interested
> in aiding Tibet, the Dalai Lama, convinced of the uselessness
> of resistance, sent a peace delegation to China in late Decem-
> ber, 1950. In May 1951, a 17-Point Agreement was signed be-
> tween the two nations. The agreement brought to an end the
> Tibetan independence which had survived since 1912 without
> ever receiving *de jure* recognition. (Karan, 1976: 17)

After the signing of the treaty, which gave China military control of the country but guaranteed Tibetan self-rule under the leadership of the Dalai Lama, new plans and programs for schools, roads, and other modern improvements were implemented. In 1954 the Dalai Lama was given 6 months' tour of China so that he might encounter at firsthand the ideals, practices, and benefits of Maoism and Marxist-Leninism; to this day, he, and many young Tibetans as well, find much that is praiseworthy in the reforms brought about by Chairman Mao.

But the initial wooing of Tibet by China, complete with silver dollars literally thrown at Tibetan people gratis (Dawa Norbu, 1974: 125), was soon over. Thousands of Tibetan children have been sent to schools in China against their parents' wishes. The development of Tibet-based light industries has primarily served to benefit the Han settlers, while Tibetans themselves have been complaining for two decades about the constant threat of starvation. The country itself has become an active military base that is "strategically very important to China—a superb defensive bastion to the southwest, through which run vital supply lines to the threatened frontier in Sinkiang" (Denwood, 1975: 17). According to reports attributed to Indian and Hongkong sources (the first, ultimately linked to U.S. and British military analysts; the second, to the pro-Taiwan *Hongkong Times*), "China has practically completed the construction of a giant nuclear base in the recesses of Tibet from which it is expected to carry out launchings of inter-continental ballistic missiles (ICBM's) as well as tests for developing nuclear war-heads for the ICBM's" (*Tibetan Review*, 1978a: 19; see also *Tibetan Review*, 1980a). Finally, most threatening of all from the perspective of cultural identity has been what Tibetans perceive as Han colonialism. In the words of the Dalai Lama, "The Chinese began to oppress the Tibetan people and to turn Tibet into a Chinese colony with total disregard for the religious, cultural and national sentiments of the people" (Dalai Lama XIV, 1969: 14).

Such opinions, shared universally by the Tibetan community in exile, are supported, from the Tibetan point of view, by reports that have been coming out of Tibet since 1959. Thus Tibetans in India have had various noncovert means of keeping informed about events and policies in Tibet: official (Tibetan government-in-exile) interviews of newly arrived refugees; conversations (in Nepal) with traders who are permitted to cross the China-Nepal border; short-wave broadcasts from Radio Lhasa, which can be monitored in north India; news items appearing in the world press; and recently, conversations with Tibetans from Tibet who are very gradually being permitted to visit—for a brief and carefully specified time controlled by threats of withholding food rations to remaining family members in Tibet— relatives now living in India. In addition, four official delegations from the Tibetan government-in-exile have been sent to Tibet for what appears to be a testing-of-the-waters by both Peking and Dharamsala. Finally, a small number of "ordinary" Tibetans living in India and abroad have also been permitted to enter Tibet for a brief time to visit their families there.[9]

As for the Lhasa uprising itself, the following chronology of the main events of March 1959 will serve to conclude this historical summary; its source is a special commemorative issue of *Tibetan Review* (1969b), which also includes eyewitness accounts, photographs, and more detailed descriptions of *rang-dbang sger-langs* ("the uprising for freedom"), the archetype of the Tibetan people's attempt to achieve independence. The following documentation reproduces the *Tibetan Review* account almost verbatim (with minor explanations added in brackets). I present it here in full as a reference for the Tibetan refugees' remembered tradition, which is the basis for my attempt at interpreting the present-day commemoration of this event by these refugees around the world.

> March 7:
>
> The Chinese Political Commissar, T'an Kuan-san, presses for a definite date in response to a previously issued invitation to the Dalai Lama to attend a theatrical performance at the Chinese Military Headquarters. The Dalai Lama agrees to March 10.
>
> March 9:
>
> The Chinese impose conditions for the Dalai Lama's attendance the next day: no Tibetan soldiers or police are to be posted along the way; the Dalai Lama is to come without the customary retinue of officials or escort of the Kusung (*sku-srung*) Regiment. By evening word spreads to Lhasa,

---

9. For descriptions of current conditions in Tibet, see the regularly featured "Tibet News" section of *Tibetan Review* as well as Fraser (1981).

causing mounting anxiety for the safety of the Dalai Lama
as the people suspect a Chinese plot to kidnap him.
March 10:
Crowds begin streaming into Norbu Lingka ["Jewel Park";
the grounds surrounding the Dalai Lama's summer palace
outside the city of Lhasa] at dawn and by late morning ten to
thirty thousand Tibetans surround the palace. A Tibetan col-
laborator is stoned to death. Repeated attempts to pacify the
crowd fail until the people are assured that the Dalai Lama
will not accept the Chinese invitation. Posting volunteers as
guards, the crowd stages a demonstration to march through
the city shouting slogans.
March 11:
A public meeting attended by all sections of the people is
held at the Government Printing Press at Shöl, below the
Potala [the Dalai Lama's palace in Lhasa, the symbol of the
Tibetan government and nation for 300 years]. The meeting
unanimously presses demands for a formal declaration of Tibetan independence and the removal of Chinese from Tibet.
March 12–16:
Public meetings and demonstrations are held in almost continuous session. Monks from neighboring monasteries and
villages from the surrounding countryside join in the protest. The Chinese keep off the streets but reports of massive
preparations and arrivals of reinforcements come from
all sides.
March 17:
At 4:00 P.M. two mortar shells fired from a nearby Chinese
camp land in Norbu Lingka. Amidst rumours of imminent
large-scale Chinese attack, the Cabinet persuades the Dalai
Lama to leave Lhasa. At dusk the Dalai Lama slips out of the
palace in disguise.
March 19:
The women of Lhasa organize a mammoth rally at the foot
of the Potala and stage mass demonstrations in the city.
A delegation of women requests the Indian and Nepalese
Consul-Generals to witness their demands to the Chinese.
March 20:
At 2:00 A.M. the Chinese begin bombarding Norbu Lingka.

March 21–22:

Valiant and desperate fighting by unorganized and ill-equipped freedom fighters against Chinese artillery, machine guns and tanks.

March 23:

By the fourth day of fighting, the last pockets of resistance in Lhasa are overcome. Meanwhile in Delhi Mr. Nehru expresses concern about the situation in Tibet and the safety of the Dalai Lama in a statement in the Indian Parliament.

March 28:

China breaks a long silence on the Tibet situation by announcing the suppression of the uprising and dissolution of the Tibetan Cabinet. . . . The Dalai Lama and the Cabinet formally proclaim a Provisional Government at Lhuntse Dzong, about three days' journey from the Indian border.

March 31:

The Dalai Lama reaches the Indian check-post at Chuthangmo in the evening.

This symbolically loaded chain of events was soon followed by the mass exodus of Tibetans from all walks of life, and by May 20, the first group of refugees to follow the Dalai Lama had arrived at Bomdila, India. From that point on, Tibetans too have been numbered among the world's uprooted and stateless populations.[10] Two decades later, the cultural threat to these people's continued existence as Tibetans is, if anything, greater than ever.

The Dalai Lama: Summarizing Symbol

Of all the elements of Tibetan tradition that survive today, none is more critical to Tibetan self-definition than the Dalai

---

10. Other research on Tibetan refugees includes Corlin (1975); M. Goldstein (1968, 1975b); Messerschmidt (1976) and Ott-Marti (1971, 1976). More general studies of refugee life and problems include Keller (1975), who focuses specifically on India (Punjabi refugees from Pakistan), as well as two significant works written in the years following the Second World War: Murphy (1955) and Schechtman (1963). For a summary of these studies, see Nowak (1978b: 35–39). In addition, a doctoral dissertation by a Tibetan, Tenzing Chhodak (1981: vi), directly addresses the following research objectives: (1) to establish the institutional objectives for Tibetan schools; (2) to identify

Lama. In his own words, which represent his reflections before leaving Tibet and his lack of fear at dying at the hands of the Chinese, the present Dalai Lama (1962) has expressed his awareness of what he means to his people:

> I felt then as I always feel, that I am only a mortal being and an instrument of the never dying spirit of my Master, and that the end of one mortal frame is not of any great consequence. But I knew my people and the officials of my government could not share my feeling. To them the person of the Dalai Lama was supremely precious. They believed the Dalai Lama represented Tibet and the Tibetan way of life, something dearer to them than anything else. They were convinced that if my body perished at the hands of the Chinese, the life of Tibet would also come to an end. (p. 195)

The crucial nature of sacred continuity in this institution, made all the more significant now by Tibetans' fear for even the ordinary continuity of their culture, is well grounded in Tibetan metaphysical theory. According to Buddhist teachings, a bodhisattva is a being who has achieved enlightenment, but who has chosen, for motives of compassion, to postpone his final entry into Nirvana until all sentient beings have been liberated from the misery of phenomenal existence. The Dalai Lama is an emanation (an incarnation) of Tibet's patron bodhisattva Avalokiteshvara (*spyan-ras-gzigs*), who has, since mythical times, been reborn in a series of culture heroes (including the greatest of the early kings). The relatively modern succession of Dalai Lamas (an unbroken line of religious-political leaders beginning with the fifteenth-century nephew and disciple of Tshong-kha-pa, Dge-'dun grub-pa) continues this lineage in contemporary times. Thus the Dalai Lama is at one and the same time a direct reincarnation of his immediate predecessor (strongly immanent sacrality) and an indirect incarnation of Avalokiteshvara (primarily transcendent sacrality).

Whatever the degree of his personal charisma (and in the case of the fifth and the thirteenth, it was considerable; in other cases,

---

general curriculum conditions in these schools; (3) to determine the extent to which the schools are presently reaching the established objectives; and (4) to present recommendations for curriculum and instructional improvement and for change in the administration.

much less so), the institutionalized or "routinized" charisma of each Dalai Lama was guaranteed once the individual had been properly identified and legitimated as the true reincarnation:

> Mere humans could not by themselves properly determine the incarnation, and the institutionalization depended on supplying the selection process with supernatural supports. The speeches and comments of a late Dalai Lama would be examined for any possible clues as to where he would be reborn. Other unusual occurrences, such as strange cloud formations or the shifting of the position of the corpse of the late Dalai Lama toward a particular direction, were analyzed by high Lamas, oracles, the Regent, and high-ranking officials. The Regent and other high dignitaries also visited a holy lake (*lha-mo'i bla-mtsho*) in which visions were traditionally seen concerning the Dalai Lama's rebirth. All of these preliminary examinations of cryptic, supernatural signs ended in the sending out by the Regent of one or more search parties composed of government officials and high Lamas to areas deemed probable places where the Dalai Lama would return to Tibet. In these areas the parties would examine stories of wondrous or strange births of children in the proper age category and finally would administer a series of tests to the prospective candidates, the children and their parents not being forewarned that they were considering the boy for the Dalai Lama. These tests consisted of showing the candidates several pairs of articles, e.g. rosaries or walking sticks, one of which had been the personal possession of the late Dalai Lama. The child was expected to choose the late Dalai Lama's things, thereby proving that he had residual knowledge of his past life, the ability to recall the events of one's past life being a characteristic of bodhisattvas and buddhas. On the basis of the reports sent by the one or more search parties, the Regent, after consulting with high Lamas and government officials, would inform the Assembly of the situation and guided by the Regent they would accept the candidate as Dalai Lama. (M. Goldstein, 1968: 162–163)

The extraordinariness of each Dalai Lama, then, comes from the fact and the continuity of each particular reincarnation, and the actual breakthrough of this sacredness into the realm of ordinary human life demands official and public ratification. Once the young boy has been "discovered" and "proven," however, his charisma has been established for the duration of his lifetime; his validating action —the correct and properly verified remembrance of people and objects from his immediate past life—makes it unnecessary for him to perform any subsequent miracles. Nonetheless, Tibetans do tend to credit the Dalai Lama with thaumaturgic powers—extraordinary knowledge more often than deeds—simply by logical deduction: if he is an incarnation of Avalokiteshvara, then he must have superhuman abilities.

Using a different system of ideas to interpret this institution, the centrality of the Dalai Lama in Tibetan culture is no less evident. Balandier, in his chapter on religion and power (1972/1967: 99– 122), makes a number of general observations that are strikingly applicable here. In considering the sacrality of power, particularly as manifested in the sacred sovereign, he regards this kind of ruler as "the repository of ultimate values" (p. 99), whose sacralized power is linked "not so much to the mortal person of the sovereign as to a function that is declared to be eternal" (p. 102). This power and this sacrality are both "profoundly ambiguous"; they are both based "on a dual polarity: that of the pure and the impure, that of the 'organizing' (and just) power and the 'violent' (and constraining or contesting) power" (p. 108). Finally, the identification of the sacred and the political "means that opposition to power (but not to its holders) is sacrilegious" (p. 106–107); thus subjects are bound to the sovereign by "a veneration or total submission that cannot be justified by reason (p. 99).

In the case of the Dalai Lama, the political aspects of this institution have been well described by M. Goldstein (1973): it functions to distribute power more widely across Tibetan society. No Dalai Lama after the "Great Fifth" has come from an aristocratic background. After each enthronement, however, the Dalai Lama's natal family would be raised to the highest ranks of the nobility, a status heritable by future generations. More specifically, the cultural role of political succession by reincarnation, interacting with the technoenvironmental matrix in which it existed, that is, the absence of new sources of economically viable agricultural land, served to generate "an inevitable circulation of estates," which in turn produced the political competition and conflict that were characteristic of the traditional Tibetan political system at any synchronic point in time" (M. Goldstein, 1973: 455; 445).

According to the dialectic rule of Tibetan religious-political theory, such "impure" and "violent" contestations for power would be balanced by this institution's "pure," "just," and "organizing" aspects; in fact, for centuries the Tibetan government, with the Dalai Lama at its apex, has been characterized as *chos-srid zung-'brel*, that is, one based on "religion and politics combined."

Given this understanding, the Dalai Lama can certainly be interpreted in the light of this designation by Ortner (1973):

> Summarizing symbols . . . are those symbols which are seen as summing up, expressing, representing for the participants in an emotionally powerfully and relatively undifferentiated way, what the system means to them. This category is essentially the category of sacred symbols in the broadest sense, and includes all those items which are objects of reverence and/or catalysts of emotion. . . . The American flag, for example, for certain Americans, stands for something called "the American way," a conglomerate of ideas and feelings including (theoretically) democracy, free enterprise, hard work, competition, progress, national superiority, freedom, etc. And it stands for them all at once. It does not encourage reflection on the logical consequences of them as they are played out in social actuality, over time and history. On the contrary, the flag encourages a sort of all-or-nothing allegiance to the whole package. . . . And this is the point about summarizing symbols in general—they operate to compound and synthesize a complex system of ideas, to "summarize" them under a unitary form which, in an old-fashioned way, "stands for" the system as a whole. (pp. 1339–1340)

The evocative strength of this particular type of symbol, however, is directly counterposed by a corresponding vulnerability: the all-or-nothing, unitary character of a summarizing symbol allows little possibility for adaptive reformulations when the social matrix that originally produced it undergoes radical change. The present Dalai Lama, His Holiness Tenzin Gyatso, who has impressed even non-Buddhists with his realism and openness to democracy and change, has given his avowed pledge to respect the will of the Tibetan people regarding the continuation of the political aspect of the institution. What he has said, in this respect, is that, if and when Tibet regains independence, he will willingly and completely relinquish the power and prerogatives of a Dalai Lama to a popularly elected leader, and toward this end he has already promulgated a draft constitution which, if ratified in Tibet, would make him virtually a figurehead (*Tibetan Review*, 1976e).

But no Tibetans, not even the most vocal critics of the Dharamsala government-in-exile, want to see this happen; for all, regardless of their sentiments toward secular power holders, feel a very real need for the one flesh-and-blood Tibetan symbol that can transcend the potentially destructive factionalism of merely human political groupings. In 1976 the worldwide Tibetan community was deeply upset by indications that His Holiness might end the lineage of Dalai Lamas, a piece of news conveyed both traditionally through the prophecies of the State (Nechung) Oracle and through the modern medium of a BBC television interview with the Dalai Lama, which had been broadcast the previous November. In that interview, His Holiness had stated that "most probably" he would be the last Dalai Lama, for he doubted that the office could continue to be beneficial to the Tibetan people much longer in view of present political realities. Then, in the first week of March 1976, the oracle made its prediction to the monks of Drepung monastery (reestablished in Karnataka State, south India): "The Dali Lama will not be in your midst much longer." At the subsequent March 10 commemoration of the Lhasa uprising (an annual event of great importance throughout the Tibetan refugee community), the Dalai Lama gave his customary address to the Tibetan public; but instead of reading his prepared speech, he spoke extemporaneously, at one point castigating his fellow Tibetans for "indulging in squabbles and factionalism" and for "desiring and emulating the luxury life styles of other rich people" (English translation presented in *Tibetan Review*, 1976c).

Soon after the March 10 address, the Dalai Lama refused the symbolic gifts (an image of the Buddha, a copy of the scriptures, and an image of a stupa, representing the Buddhist triad of body, speech, and mind) of the *brtan-bzhugs* ("invitation to long life") ceremony his followers tried to offer on his behalf; he then went on a 3-month retreat. Subsequent developments (i.e., the Dalai Lama's return to a "normal" leadership role) have been explained by the Dalai Lama himself as indicating that "the danger which existed now seems to be over" (*Tibetan Review*, 1977a: 23), but the actual basis of this "danger" has never been clarified, and the drama itself brought forth a discussion yet to be concluded. The strongly expressed words of one young Tibetan I spoke with were met with ready agreement every time I requoted them to others: "His Holiness has no right to end the line. We need him far more than any god."

Be it summarizing symbol or reincarnation of Avalokiteshvara that underlies the theory, on this last point, anthropologist and Tibetan community are in full accord. Moreover, the intensley felt conviction Tibetans have that they need the Dalai Lama if they are to continue as a "race" or ethnic group impinges on both poles of that profound ambiguity I referred to earlier: the Dalai Lama's power is both sacred (or pure, just, and "peaceful") and profane (or political, contesting, and "violent"). Given the sociopolitical realities of life these stateless refugees must experience daily, it is no accident that the leader they revere is, to them, neither wholly transcendent (and thereby out of this world) nor wholly immanent (enmeshed in temporalities like the rest of us), but an ambiguous symbol imbued with the qualities of both. In ways that I detail later in this book, Tibetans use this ambiguity; they attempt to make sense of a government-in-exile that is de facto but not de jure by, among other strategies, fervently reemphasizing a centuries-old religious-political institution—the Dalai Lama as supreme ruler of Tibet—that was never meant to be bounded by the laws of this world alone.

With respect to my own attempts to interpret this situation, the cultural traditions I recognize as mine likewise include experience with church/state symbiosis. Having been brought up not only Catholic, but Polish Catholic, I, like the Tibetans, was quite familiar with the implications of nationalism in the guise of religious identity. Poland, too, had once disappeared from world maps as an independent state. From 1795 to 1918 the Catholic church in that nation provided the primary means for Poles to continue to define themselves as "Polish," as distinct from the Protestant Austrians and Prussians and the Orthodox Russians who had partitioned their country. The present situation vis-à-vis the Soviet Union, highlighted even more by a Polish pope, only increases the parallels between my own religious-ethnic history and that of the Tibetans, whose Buddhist faith and Dalai Lama leader stand quintessentially for their nationality over and against that of the communist Chinese.

In addition to that mutually discovered instance of commonality in our respective religious-ethnic backgrounds, my Tibetan interlocutors and I also shared several interrelated experiences: childhood impressions of the smell of incense, still-vivid memories of church or temple interiors made as ornate as possible, and all the related arguments for and against spending money on cathedrals while the poor are starving. Long, earnest discussions on such topics more than once ended with my Tibetan counterparts getting to know at least as much about me and my cultural tradition as the reverse. Attempting to write about such discussions in my diary, I would wonder how a dissertation could come out of such introspection. It is probably another aspect of my cultural tradition that I would worry about self-knowledge and reflection being rather useless as "data."

Rangzen and March 10: Root Metaphor and Key Scenario

While Tibetan tradition supporting the institution of the Dalai Lama extends back at least six centuries, the two contemporary symbols I have indentified in Tibetan refugee culture[11]—*rangzen* (the newly evolving metaphor), and its behavioral counterpart, the annual commemoration of the Lhasa uprising—are both primarily the result of late-twentieth-century events, ideology, and experience.

The Tibetan term for *independence, rangzen* (pronounced raŋtseen;[12] spelled *rang-btsan* in Tibetan orthography), has only recently

11. Ortner's article on key symbols (1973) distinguishes between "summarizing symbols" and "elaborating symbols," the latter category being further divided into "root metaphors" (essentially cognitive in character) and "key scenarios" (typically involving behavioral elements). When I first began to analyze the Dalai Lama and the *rangzen* complex as symbols, I was struck by the great applicability of her categorizations to my data. In the present work, however, I pay less attention to the distinction between root metaphor and key scenario, choosing instead to treat "independence" as a contemporary, secular motif having both cognitive and behavioral manifestations and implications.
12. See M. Goldstein's dictionary (1975a: 24) for the phonetic values of the transcription used here.

been introduced into the Tibetan lexicon. When the Chinese first began their attempts at indoctrinating the Tibetan population after 1949, Tibetan vocabulary at the time was, of course, replete with hundreds of terms relevant to topics of metaphysics, philosophy, religion, and depth psychology. There were, however, no standard Tibetan words for such modern political concepts as "independence," "exploitation," "socialism," "capitalism," and so on. Accordingly, newly needed terminology was created by loan translation. The neologism *rangzen*, for example, was coined by compounding already existing Tibetan morphemes: *rang*, meaning "self," and *btsan*, meaning "power."

The first element in the Tibetan term *rang* is quite straightforward in its denotation and usage; it can occur alone as a free morpheme, and it also occurs as the first syllable in scores of binomial compounds formed according to the general pattern of "one's own *N*," or "self-*N*." By contrast, the second morpheme, *btsan*, has a much more evocative range of meanings. Its primary denotation is "power" or "force," but a look at compounds built with this syllable reveals that this particular kind of power is aggressive, compelling, and even violent in nature. Thus the morpheme *btsan* appears in such Tibetan terms as *btsan-rgyal ring-lugs* ("imperialism"), *btsan-gnon* ("oppression"), *btsan-'dzul* ("invasion"), and interestingly enough from our perspective, *btsan-byol-pa* (literally, "one who has escaped from oppression"), which is one of several Tibetan words for *refugee*.

It is also instructive to note the difference in connotation between *rang-btsan* and its closest synonym, *rang-dbang*, which Tibetans translate as "freedom." The morpheme *dbang* also means "power," but this latter kind of power is that of legitimized authority rather than forceful coercion; thus the Tibetan phrase *dbang-skur* (literally, "to bestow power," which can be translated as "consecration" or "initiation") has in fact a religious acceptation. The official Tibetan name for the March 10 commemoration employs the *dbang*, or "legitimate," rather than the *btsan*, or "aggressive," morpheme for power; the complete phrase is *rang-dbang sger-langs* ("the uprising for freedom:"). On the other hand, the name of the most militant youth magazine is *Rangzen*, a term that is also the impelling watchword of Tibetan political consciousness.

One final observation can likewise be made in this connection, although no definitive conclusion can be drawn from it: the word *btsan*, which in ancient times indicated "a most important class of Tibetan deities (or demons)" (Haarh, 1969: 78), appears in the names of 17 of the 32 kings traditionally associated with the prehistoric Yarlung dynasty (Haarh, 1979: 40), and it is also present in the names of the three greatest Dharma-rajas (or *chos-rgyal*, the Tibetan kings who most supported Buddhism) in Tibetan historical tradition: Srong-btsan sgam-po, Khri-srong lde-btsan, and Khri-gtsug lde-btsan (Ral-pa-can). In terms of its primary referent (independence in the strictly political sense), the word *rangzen* is thus replete with semantic as well as historical connotative possibilities.

In investigating the metaphorical associations of this term, however, evidence of innovation should not be sought in dictionaries or historical texts, but in the ongoing social situation. According to Ortner's (1973) classification, root metaphors are key symbols that "operate to sort out experience, to place it in cultural categories, and to help us think about how it all hangs together" (p. 1341). The one experience that has most fundamentally touched the lives of all Tibetan refugees has indeed prompted thoughtful attempts at sense making. In their own words: "We have lost our country, but someday we will regain our independence."

In the analysis that follows, I am most concerned with this concept of independence as a *meta*political image, that is, as a metaphor suggestive of a range of meanings going beyond the notion of political autonomy. Over and above their situation of statelessness, two critical problems face Tibetan refugees today: that of self-definition (either as individuals vis-à-vis other Tibetans or as Tibetans vis-à-vis the rest of the world) and that of de facto and de jure relationships of power (again, in reference to life both within and beyond the Tibetan community). For such people, the goal of achieving *rangzen*, with all its potential associations of independence equaling "self-power," is indeed a polysemic one.

As for the behavioral implications of this essentially cognitive metaphor, it is in this connection that the annual commemoration of the Lhasa uprising can best be understood: the events that took place in Tibet in March 1959, have become, for refugees, the *illud tempus*, or archetype, that sustains a recurrent but deeply meaningful new secular ritual.

Many of the activities repeated annually by Tibetans on March 10 can be seen as a reenactment or reaffirmation of key elements of the original drama that took place in Lhasa in March 1959: the mass rally outside the Dalai Lama's palace; the converging of monks and villagers from the surrounding monasteries and countryside; the threat, or actual outbreak of violence (in addition to the impending attack by the Chinese, a collaborater was stoned to death); the city-wide protest march and shouting of slogans; public meetings; and finally, two nonrepeatable events: the formal proclamation of a provisional Tibetan government (March 28, 1959) and the arrival of the Dalai Lama in India (March 31, 1959).

Present-day March 10 commemorations, which are held all over the world wherever there is a sufficiently large Tibetan population, employ most if not all of these same elements. A crowd gathers in a central, public location; speeches are made; and a vociferous demonstration takes place, marked by conspicuous wearing of national dress, singing of the national anthem, ubiquitous display of the Tibetan flag, pictures of the Dalai Lama, as well as slogans, banners, and placards proclaiming the Tibetan case against the Chinese. In addition, the two happenings that could occur but once historically are also affirmed. The Dalai Lama delivers an annual March 10 address (in places other than Dharamsala, his prewritten speech is read out by a local Tibetan official); and the theme of India, the host country, is played up by frequent mention of the long centuries of Indo-Tibetan historical ties and friendly relations.

Whether the demonstration takes place in New Delhi, Madras, New York City, or Zurich, it almost always includes a march or procession from one significant point in the city to another, with the route as well as beginning and end points carefully selected to insure maximum publicity for the Tibetan cause. In 1969, for example, demonstrators in Delhi marched from a Tibetan Buddhist temple to Rajghat, a pilgrimage site near the sacred Jamuna River where Ghandi was cremated, where they publicly "reaffirmed their faith in the teachings of Mahatma Gandhi" (*Tibetan Review*, 1969a: 4). A recounting of this event as celebrated in south India (M. Goldstein, 1975b: 22) mentions another of its important features: the slogans, placards, banners, and speeches are written or spoken in English, Hindi, or other local languages. Clearly the afirmation of national "self" is done with great concern for ethnic "other."

A final indication of deliberate impression management can be noted in the message of the verbal media: in India, the speeches, posters, and placards all place great emphasis on the mutuality of Indo-Tibetan relations, from the perspective of both ideology (recalling the long centuries of shared religious traditions) and pragmatism (pointing out how a free and neutral Tibet could serve as a buffer state between India and China).

As a key scenario, then, this dramatic sequence of actions very definitely serves to affirm national identity over and against the fact of statelessness. In a March 10 address given less than 10 years after the original event, the Dalai Lama himself emphasized this element of "us versus them." While his words were meant to refer to the archetype itself, they are certainly relevant to the present-day reenactment as well: "It was that fateful day which united the whole country in defiance of the Chinese and re-declared our sense of nationhood in no uncertain terms to the outside world, and that struggle to assert ourselves as a people still continues today both inside and outside of Tibet" (quoted in *Tibetan Review*, 1968a: 8). With such a repertoire of symbolic elements, the March 10 commemoration can indeed be seen as a key scenario, that is, as a ritual that publicly dramatizes both an ideal goal (proudly affirmed national identity) and the strategy for achieving it (self-conscious proclamation of "Tibetanness" to and in the midst of others who are not Tibetan).

Both the *rangzen* metaphor and the March 10 commemoration may thus be interpreted as relatively new creations engendered by people threatened by the loss of old certainties. In attempting to rescue, revivify, and even create anew whatever meanings would now be viable in their new situation, Tibetans have very definitely had to confront the fact of severed connections, gaps between the familiar and the alien, and multiple images of who they are and who they should be.

As I myself try to interpret all this, I, too, cannot avoid being caught up in the hall of mirrors. I, too, on an individual level, in any case, need to create new structures of meaning, new ways of defining myself for myself and others, for I too must encounter the self or "myself" that is being reflected back at me in the course of these intercultural and interpersonal interactions, refracted into multiple images (now American, now female, now Polish, now doctoral candidate, now friend, now something else). For both the Tibetans and for me, such recently crafted props for meaning (new combinations and alterations of self-referential labels, identities, and strategies) are bound to be imperfect and unfinished. Moreover, if they are to be at all open and therefore capable of being reformulated in response to changes in the social matrix, these creations must be marked by a significant degree of ambiguity.

My Situation as Anthropologist: Fieldwork and Other Contingencies

The location and time of my fieldwork experience can be recounted quite simply. On the other hand, the circumstances that prompted me to take this rather than that turn—both literally, in the geographic sense, and figuratively, in the sense of theoretical focus, relationships to particular Tibetan persons, and self-monitoring of the actual writing process—are not simply evaluative choices that sprang up ex nihilo. Rather, they are definitely rooted in the contingencies of my existential situation.

To begin with the most explicit conditions of my research: The present study is based on fieldwork I did in north India, where I was a junior fellow of the American Institute of Indian Studies for approximately 10 months, from September 1976 through June 1977. During this time I spent 7½ months at my primary research site, a school and foster homes complex that together served approximately 1,000 Tibetan children and young adults from ages 5 to about 20. In addition, I also spent 1½ months with Tibetan university and college students at my first place of residence, a modern Indian city whose university served as my official home base under the terms of my grant. My travels through India enabled me to meet and interview Tibetans living and studying in Delhi, at a girls' college in Simla, at a Tibetan institute of higher studies in Varanasi (Sarnath), and at a Tibetan day school and settlement in south India in Bylakuppe. Also, in the course of three trips to Dharamsala, the Tibetan capital-in-exile, I visited and interviewed teachers and students from the Tibetan Children's Village; the Tibetan Music, Dance and Drama Society (now the Tibetan Institute of Performing Arts); the Buddhist School of Dialectics; and the Tibetan Astro-Medical Centre.

But this quasi-simple recounting, supported, of course, by the de rigueur statement that I obtained my information via the standard anthropological techniques of participant observation and directed as well as open-ended interviews, already conceals some contingencies that have greatly influenced the topic and the writing of this particular book. My original research proposal, anxiously written and rewritten in the fall of 1975, concerned a subject that was in fact quite different from what I actually did study. I had wanted to do research on Tibetan folklore, particularly the present-day transmission of the *Gesar* epic, but the circumstances of my stay in India, especially the fact that I never once encountered any Tibetan specialists or bards of this genre, made this impossible.

According to the policy by which project and visa clearance was issued, foreigners wishing to do research in India had to be affililated with an Indian institution of higher studies; in addition, junior fellows (those doing doctoral research) were assigned an Indian professor as their supervisor, who would serve as a liaison between the student and the Government of India Ministry of Education, should the need for such ever arise. In my case, my supervisor and university of affiliation were located in a city where virtually the only Tibetans were college students. My first 6 weeks of fieldwork were thus spent with this rather untypical sample of Tibetan refugees: all spoke English, and all were young adults living away from their families and Tibetan communities while pursuing various programs of higher study.

It is in fact this group of Tibetans who convinced me that, given my situation, the richest lode I could mine would not be folklore, but rather education, particularly the Tibetan primary and secondary systems they had just left. The evolution of my dissertation topic thus owes much to the earliest Tibetan friends and acquaintances, for it was also at their suggestion that I made an exploratory trip to the Tibetan residential school most of them had attended. It is this institution that then became the site of my fieldwork for the rest of my stay in India.

My residence there involved another series of contingencies. Because most Tibetan schools operate under the jurisdiction of the Government of India Ministry of Education, they are subject to its regulations; the latter organization can and does prohibit foreigners from observing in the classrooms when school is in session. But in addition to the school itself, my research site also included a second institution: a foster homes complex for over 600 Tibetan orphans and children of destitute parents. This latter institution consisted at the time of 25 individual homes modeled after the Pestallozi Children's Village (a home and school in Trogen, Switzerland, originally established for children orphaned by the Second World War) and was staffed by 25 Tibetan couples who serve as foster parents. This institution is privately funded (chiefly by donations of individuals and charitable organizations from all over the world), so its own primary school is not subject to Indian government restrictions on foreign visitors. Thus my classroom observations were mainly confined to this school, which includes two levels of kindergarten plus grades 1 and 2. In addition, for a brief period (barely 2 weeks) I coached tenth- and eleventh-grade students who were reviewing, during winter vacation, for the All-India Higher Secondary Examination; and finally, I also observed in the middle and upper grades of another privately funded Tibetan school elsewhere in north India.

My specific method of participant observation in the Tibetan-language classes involved a fortuitous combination of actual and explainable goals and purposes. Before coming to India, I had studied Tibetan languge and literature at the University of Washington, but the script I had learned to write was *dbu-can*, a style that Tibetans regard somewhat as Westerners would regard machine-produced printing: eminently readable, but rarely reproduced as a handwriting style. The cursive script they do use in writing, however—*dbu-med*—is taught right from primary school. Thus I could quite honestly introduce myself to the Tibetan langauge teachers as a student interested in learning what they were teaching: cursive Tibetan script. This explanation was readily understood by all. Tibetans in India are familiar with Westerners studying their religion and language in special courses set up for them in Dharamsala, and my request to become part of daily classroom routine caused no real disturbance once the initial novelty of an overgrown "English" student passed into matter-of-fact acceptance. In no time, I had a working relationship with the students who sat near me. When I could not quite decipher the teacher's handwriting on the blackboard, they would explain it to me letter by letter, and when they felt like making sotto voce comments about anything under the sun, I was always included in the audience.

What resulted from this very fortunate but unplanned connection with a residential school, then, was a very skewed sample of ages and kin groups: the community where I lived, including teachers' and administrators' families, had fewer than 50 married couples, but over 1,000 children, most of them orphans, and almost all of them living at the homes foundation or in dormitories, under the supervision of Tibetan houseparents. Some 300 of these children did have their own families elsewhere in India; these were the boarders who had been sent to the schools by their parents, who at the time were paying 100 rupees (about U.S. $13) per month for their food, lodging, and clothing. In addition, the student population also included about 100 local day students who attended classes either at the government-sponsored school or the privately endowed primary school, but these were the only Tibetan children in the area who lived with their families.[13] The vast majority of the people I lived and conversed with were thus children and young adults living outside normally constituted (nuclear or extended) Tibetan family life. As a foreigner complying with Indian restrictions, I was never able to be a participant observer in a more regular situation for any prolonged length of time.

Because of all these circumstances, then, my fieldwork evolved in a quite different direction from that of my original plans. First, it soon became apparent to me that I would have to readjust significantly the focus of my intended research. Accordingly, I chose the general topic of education and culture change, all the moreso as this particular problem, which I *could* investigate in my fieldwork situation, was, by their own admission, of great concern to Tibetans themselves.

Second, my all-too-close brush with real panic at the thought of lacking both topic and field site indefinitely certainly affected more than the redefinition of my topic. Hermeneutic concepts such as "distanciation" and "appropriation," which I had heretofore consid-

13. I should also point out that a comparatively small number of Tibetan students, who are either from relatively wealthy families or are privately sponsored by a foreign benefactor, attend much more prestigous private elementary and secondary schools, many founded by British missionaries during the time of the British Raj. Although my fieldwork did not involve me in this setting at all, it is worth noting that the graduates of these schools comprise a disproportionately high percentage of spokesmen for the Tibetan cause (the exclusively masculine referent is intended).

ered only theoretically, suddenly took on a very real significance in the light of my now-critical need to communicate with these "others." Likewise, the problem of overcoming cultural estrangement, which in hermeneutics refers to the interpretation of written texts from a past era, also characterized my own situation, for I, too, was faced with the necessity of "rescuing meaning" in more ways than one. In fact, now that I reflect on my fieldwork experience from this side of the spatial-temporal-cultural gap that separates me from them, the concept of tradition appears central to the whole research endeavor. In investigating my ultimate topic—the development of new and adapted symbolic forms among the young generation of Tibetans educated in modern India—problems of cultural transmission, ontological and epistemological assumptions, and sociocultural change in Tibetan society were, of course, critical underlying factors, but these same issues have been no less crucial in shaping the tradition in my society of doing anthropological fieldwork and then writing up and publishing the findings.[14]

At the most personal level, the implications of all of this for my research experience can begin with the question Who were the "I" and the "they" who were mutually interacting and affecting each other? Part of the answer emerged quite naturally in the course of regular day-to-day contact. The Tibetans who befriended me realized before too long that I was neither a rich benefactor or sponsor for a refugee child nor a Western dharma freak (two common categories for "European" visitors). My photographs and conversations about my family and friends at home served to establish my credentials as a genuine human being, and my structural position in India—as a woman alone in a country where Tibetans, too, consider themselves foreigners—brought forth anecdotes of their own about "what it means to be non-Indian here." On my part, I found myself reaching back into my own past for memories and impressions that would likewise be mutually meaningful. I had grown up during the years of melting-pot ideology in a neighborhood where "our" grocers were just as likely to count change in Polish as in English, and I remember defining myself ethnically, in "pluralistic" America, at age

14. More and more attention is now being given to this general problem of fieldwork as cultural activity in and of itself; see, for example, Rabinow (1977). For a further discussion of other representative works in this vein, see Dumont (1978: 6–13) and Marcus and Cushman (1982).

9. My closest Tibetan friends shared and reciprocated such revelations of my personal history with similar disclosures of their own, reflecting personally and in particular about such problems as ethnic self-definition, the generation gap, and changing religious beliefs and practices. For other Tibetans—the more impersonally known "informants" of anthropological jargon—such a presentation of self on my part served likewise to add a definite plus to the rapport between us.

At a broader level of consideration, however, this whole process of ongoing, dialectic interpretation between a particular "me" and a particular "them" may also be taken as a metonym for the research encounter itself in a more general sense. To be sure, the implications of this last observation extend far beyond the purpose of the present book, and I make little attempt here to address all the philosophical and epistemological issues that would be relevant in this connection. Nonetheless, one aspect of this larger problem does deserve special mention vis-à-vis contemporary anthropologizing: the current concern for decolonizing anthropology must itself involve dialectic interaction. Not only must anthropologists, who are essentially Western-oriented, regardless of nationality, confront the "other" in the form of Third World attitudes, policies, and restrictions regarding social science research and goals; but in addition, the implications and assumptions of the familiar world shaped by graduate school colleagues and training, expectations about Ph.D. committees and future publications, and even the process of reentry home from the field are also becoming increasingly better known to "them," the "natives."

In recounting the particular contingencies of my fieldwork experience, I in no way intend to convey the impression that my problems finding a workable site and topic were unique or even unusual for an anthropologist today. Likewise, the remarks that follow are also becoming more and more applicable to research situations everywhere; for like it or not, the use of English as a world language is increasing daily, and the possibility of assuming a continued correlation of Group A with Location B is becoming more and more problematic.

With respect to my own case, then, these two factors have doubly served to augment the likelihood of mutual understanding between "them" and "me." First, I did not have to depend solely on their language for communication, but I and they could use my own as well. I have been able to rely heavily for data on English-language publications put out in India by Tibetans themselves and intended for both Tibetan and non-Tibetan audiences. These range in scope from a quarterly journal and a monthly magazine to anthologies and local newsletters published occasionally, and almost all are available abroad via subscription or on special request. On a more personal level, friendships made with individuals who can read and write one's language can continue to be nourished by regular air mail correspondence. This has the effect of radically challenging such finally dying anthropological clichés as "my people the Xs" or "the Noble (but illiterate) Savage."

The second factor adding to the possibility of we/they dialogue concerns the increasing mobility of individuals, families, and even whole communities of people who, in the past, had most likely never left or gone far from the land of their ancestors. As refugees, for example, Tibetans now live all over the world, and this includes a fair number of Tibetan intellectual specialists who, before 1959, had spent years systematically studying Tibetan philosophy, logic, and metaphysics in monastic libraries in Tibet. The current Western interest in Tibetan Buddhism, coupled with the flight of such intellectual elites from Tibet, has brought these native scholars to the forefront of Tibetan studies worldwide. Accordingly, these intellectuals from another tradition are now in a position to be recognized by non-Tibetans too for their expertise in subjects currently taught in Asian departments at various European, North American, and Japanese universities. Far from being regarded as merely fascinating or quaintly knowledgeable, the Tibetan scholars are esteemed by these non-Tibetans as genuine (rather than "exotic") intellectuals, for the criteria of excellence here are familiar to all parties concerned. On a much less arcane level as well, the very act of arranging a meeting with these individuals (mutually checking schedules, phoning ahead for directions, avoiding a parking ticket, etc.) likewise challenges the notion that "fieldwork" can only occur over there in Shangri-la. In terms of the ideal mutual regard and reciprocity that should prevail in a we/they dialogue, all of these facts are worth considering.

As for my own experience in this respect, I have twice participated in international conferences of Tibetologists, where papers were read by Tibetans and non-Tibetans alike. In addition, I have been able to share the results of my fieldwork (dissertation, conference presentations, writings, and personal reflections) with Tibetans who are now situated in such far-flung places as England, Switzerland, Germany, the San Francisco Bay area, the Pacific Northwest, and graduate schools on both the East and West Coasts. Likewise, I have been fortunate in having two Tibetan friends, both perceptive insiders in the Tibetan community in India but with comparative experience as students at British or American universities, who read and criticized my manuscript as it was being written. Moreover, the first generation of Tibetan graduate students has already begun to produce Tibetan holders of Western doctoral degrees. Personal communication with some of these people via letters, sharing of rough drafts and ideas, and exchanging of phone calls, papers, and dissertations has certainly added to my conviction that the problem of personal meaning (why we write, why we are trying to enlighten, convince, or gain approval from some academic committee, social group, or other relevant people) has at least as much effect on our research as does our shared interest in Tibetan culture. The phenomenon of the shrinking globe is indeed making it possible for more and more anthropologists like me to pick up the phone and "dial a native" to check data and interpretations. Beyond this, however, I believe that the implications of what I am describing touch the whole enterprise of contemporary anthropologizing.

In comparison with other displaced ethnic groups studied by social scientists, the situation of Tibetan refugees is probably somewhat exceptional in this respect: because of the inimitable figure and prior international reputation of the Dalai Lama, a considerable amount of international aid and attention was directed right from the start toward the goal of preserving and continuing Tibetan knowledge. Yet, in other ethnographic contexts as well, it is becoming more and more the rule rather than the exception for Western researchers to regard native intellectuals as equals at the very least, and this holds especially true for those, be they social scientists or area specialists, who have attempted a thorough study of the native language, thought, and aesthetic systems. In sum, the romantic (if not colonial) notion of fieldwork as an exotic space-time isolate, neatly bracketed apart from "the real world" by visa dates, Lomotil,

and plane tickets, is being punctured again and again by constant in-
terpenetrations of mundane realities shared, if not taken for granted,
by both them and us.

Theory, Meaning, and Reflection: The Quest for Understanding

As a means of relating symbolic and hermeneutic
theory to the main issues discussed thus far in this chapter—the
historical background of Tibetan refugees in India, the transmission
and development of new and adapted symbolic forms among the
new school-going generation, and the contingencies and implications
of my fieldwork experience—the following questions can serve to
provide a framework for systematic consideration:

1. What relationships can be identified between the general problems addressed by symbolic anthropology and the specific case
   of the Tibetan refugees in India?
2. How can the particular anthropological insights and conclusions generated by this kind of investigation be related to a
   more general theory of interpretation and meaning?
3. Considering these issues not only empirically and theoretically, but also reflexively, what does it mean to "overcome cultural estrangement"? In other words, for the anthropologist
   qua self-reflective human being, what is involved in attempting to "understand the other"?

With respect to the first question, any consideration of Tibetan
refugees from the perspective of symbolic anthropology must first
begin with a clarification of predominant focus, for this approach
is potentially concerned with a variety of issues that could all be
relevant in this particular case (e.g., problems of ethnicity, cultural
transmission, dramatic representation, the notion of power and the
sacred, and so forth; see, respectively, (1) Barth, 1969; De Vos, 1975;
De Vos and Romanucci-Ross, 1975; (2) Fortes, 1970; Mayer, 1970;
Middleton, 1970; Quillen, 1955, Wallace, 1961; (3) Burke, 1966;
Geertz, 1972; Peacock, 1968; (4) Balandier, 1972/1967; Cohen, 1976;

Heusch, 1962; Schwartz, Turner, and Tuden, 1966; Tambiah, 1977). The focus I have chosen—the deliberately fostered transmission and later adaptation of key symbolic forms (specifically, the image of the Dalai Lama and the emerging motif of *rangzen*, or "independence") among young Tibetans educated in India—does indeed touch all of these concerns; but the central point as I define it involves these people's quest for a meaningful interpretation of their present situation.

In my dissertation I made use of the concept of "liminality," which has been elaborated so thoroughly by Turner (1967, 1969a, 1969b, 1974, 1975). Specifically, I examined the possibility that this "betwixt and between" state (as Turner terms it) of belonging precisely nowhere might, with certain qualifications, also be characteristic of refugees living in exile. Having left their native land, they have entered a legal limbo in which they are citizens of no country on earth (Nowak, 1978b: 1–2, 231–237).

Turner's use of the term, however, is more narrow than mine. Following van Gennep (1960/1908), he has treated liminality as the intermediary stage of a formally structured ritual (e.g., initiation rite) or an informally structured ritual (e.g., pilgrimages or millenarian movements), where the initial stage is characterized by separation or detachment from a previous state, and the final stage involves socially recognized reaggregation or integration at a new level of definition (Turner, 1969b: 94).

In contrast to this, my use of the liminality concept differs from Turner's in three ways:

1. In a more formally structured liminal condition, the passage from former to future state, however "free" it may appear at the time, is ultimately controlled by knowledgeable specialists who have themselves undergone a similar experience. In the case of the Tibetan refugees, neither the de facto leaders of the community nor the inexperienced youth can be confident that such "reintegration" will in fact occur.

2. Whereas a rite or phase that is liminal in the strict sense of the term can well afford to cultivate ambiguity by annulling or obscuring "the classifications on which order normally depends" (Turner, 1974: 273), such is not the case for stateless refugees, whose traditional norms and rules have already been

strained and taxed by the sudden confrontation with strange new values and mores.

3. Participants in an institutionalized, clearly bounded ritual may indeed be motivated to speculate about "the difficulties that peculiarly beset their own society" (Turner, 1974: 242), for the freedom to criticize and elaborate cultural beliefs in this temporary context does not ultimately challenge the efficacy of traditional explanations once the ritual is over. For refugees, however, such searching is not a free gift of the moment, but a necessity brought on by circumstances beyond their control.

Nevertheless, once these qualifications are acknowledged, and the idea of liminality has been extended to describe the situation of a displaced and stateless ethnic group, I find Turner's (1974) comments on this condition to be very provocative indeed: Liminality "is essentially ambiguous, unsettled, and unsettling" (p. 274). Furthermore, it is also a period replete with creative possibilities, at once liberating and dangerous. "Symbols and metaphors found in abundance in liminality represent various dangerous ambiguities of this ritual stage, since the classifications on which order normally depends are annulled or obscured—other symbols designate temporary antinomic liberation from behavioral norms and cognitive rules" (p. 273). Seen in this light, then, the central point of my focus, the Tibetan refugees' quest for a meaningful interpretation of their present situation, can be related to this theoretical statement from symbolic anthropology: in ambiguous social states, symbols and metaphors are especially likely to proliferate.

In the chapters that follow, I attempt to show that the particular symbol (the Dalai Lama), metaphor (*rangzen*), and dramatic reenactment (the March 10 commemoration) I have identified all affect, and in turn are affected by, Tibetans' current struggle to make sense of their individual and social lives today. Each of these symbolic forms has to be learned, most obviously by the young generation, but also in the case of the much more recent metaphor and motif of "independence," by older Tibetans who are likewise involved in the process of being (re-)socialized.

Accordingly, I have organized the two ethnographic chapters in this way: in Chapter 2, which deals with explicit teaching, I concentrate on the transmission of traditional symbols through formal schooling. Although schools did exist in pre-1959 Tibet (primarily for those marked as actual or potential elites), the Tibetan schools sponsored by the government of India represent a radical break with past expectations concerning education. Both the form (secular rather than monastic) and the content (modern rather than traditional syllabus) of this type of cultural transmission have changed drastically, and all of this can certainly be related to the general problem of refugee adaptation. Yet these schools also emphasize some traditional cultural elements as well; and, as in the case of Tibetan religious history and language, these are positively and deliberately enshrined in the curriculum. It is in this context, as part of the goal of achieving viable cultural continuity, that the summarizing symbol of the Dalai Lama is presented and explained most carefully to Tibetan children.

In Chapter 3, on the other hand, I deal with the other manner in which symbols are learned: implicit generalization from social experience. Here, I give particular attention to the options and activities of young Tibetans after they graduate from these deliberately supportive Tibetan schools. As might be expected, the contrast between ideals ("work for our people"; "never give up your Tibetanness") and reality ("my family cannot make it economically") hits these young people hard, especially when, as individuals, they suddenly see themselves as Tibetans, working with or competing against Indians who are, after all, citizens in their own country. For them, dealing with the tension between traditional (kin- and group-centered) ideology and present-day (individualistically focused) experience involves a very necessary attempt at reinterpreting the personal and social implications of what is and what ought to be. While the explicit meanings of the *rangzen* motif and its supporting March 10 scenario are well known to every Tibetan, the possibility of additional or implicit meanings is particularly significant in this context. Especially for the young generation, struggling with problems of primary loyalties and individual and ethnic self-definition, "independence" is more than a Tibetan political goal, "properly" interpreted, it can serve as legitimation for new behavior patterns too.

With respect to the second question I posed at the beginning of this section—How can the particular anthropological insights and conclusions generated by this kind of investigation be related to a more general theory of interpretation and meaning?—the key issue, as I see it, is that of polysemy. Both the traditional symbol of the Dalai Lama and the newly emerging metaphor and dramatization of *rangzen* derive their evocative potency from the fact that they impinge on different meanings and dimensions of meaning at once: power and sacrality, self- and group affirmation, ideology and experience. This quality of semantic richness, of multiple possibilities of signification, constitutes what hermeneutics would consider a surplus of meaning; furthermore, whenever such multivocality occurs, it warrants interpretation (*"C'est le surplus initial de sens qui motive tradition et interpretation"*—Ricoeur, 1963: 614).

At the level of the *word*, polysemy involves a cumulative, metaphoric process. It is cumulative in that the word picks up new dimensions of meaning (subject to the semantic limitation that words can have multiple meanings, but not an infinite number of meanings) without losing the old ones. As a result of this cumulative process, the metaphoricity of the word is nourished; that is, the word becomes loaded with new values of usage. When polysemy would be problematic (Ricoeur gives the example of the word *volume*), it is the *context* that acts to resolve the ambiguity of the reference (for *volume*, the topics *geometry* or *library* would serve this contextualizing purpose).

In symbolic *language*, on the other hand, the polysemy of multivocalic words is freed: "Instead of sifting out one dimension, the context lets several of them pass through and indeed it consolidates several of them, which go together in the manner of texts which have been superimposed on a palimpset" (Ricoeur, 1967: 818–819, my translation). In the case of symbolic discourse, then, more than one interpretation is justified; that is, multiple dimensions of meaning are relevant and realizable at the same time.

Although Ricoeur's work mainly concerns research in his own disciplines (philosophy, theology, history, and literature), a number of symbolic anthropologists employ similar concepts in their interpretation of expressive culture or "the social use of metaphor" (Sapir and Crocker, 1977; see also Boon, 1972; Fernandez, 1974, 1977; and of course, the works of Lévi-Strauss, Turner, and Geertz). Likewise, Ricoeur (1971, 1981) himself has explicitly considered the relevance of hermeneutic interpretation of social science methodology. Using the notion of "text" as a paradigm for interpreting the "object" of the social sciences (which he takes to be "Weber's 'meaningfully oriented behavior'"), he outlines the parallels between human action and symbolic discourse, elucidating the implications for interpretation in the social sciences. From the perspective of my study, what is significant in Ricoeur's writings are his ideas about "non-ostensive references." In the context of textual interpretation, these references *beyond* the actual text constitute the text's "world," "not in the cosmological sense of the word, but in an ontological dimension" (Ricoeur, 1971: 543). Applied to the context of "meaningfully oriented behavior" (the motif of "independence" among contemporary Tibetan refugees, for example), this concept of metarelevance explains how an "important" action can develop meanings beyond its originating or immediate situation: "The meaning of an important event exceeds, overcomes, transcends, the social conditions of its production and may be reenacted in new social contexts. Its importance is its durable relevance, and in some cases, its omnitemporal relevance" (pp. 543–544). Furthermore, a symbolic action of this sort "does not only mirror its time, but it opens up a world which it bears within itself" (p. 544).

To open up a world, however, is not merely the work of symbolic anthropology or a theory of meaning in the abstract. Put simply, this phrase begs the question Who? More completely, it is not merely a question of whose world, but of who is doing the interpreting. With this in mind, then, the third and final question I raised at the beginning of this discussion is now apropos: Considering the above issues not only empirically and theoretically, but also reflexively, what does it mean "to overcome cultural estrangement"? In other words, for the anthropologist qua self-reflective human being, what is involved in attempting to understand the "other"?

Perhaps the best starting point for these considerations would be a clarification of what "understanding" in this context does *not* mean. Philosophical hermeneutics has dealt with this problem at length, and one of its chief representatives, Gadamer (1976), has written in detail about "the astounding naiveté of the subjective consciousness that, in trying to understand a text, says, 'But that is what is written here!'" (p. 121). What Gadamer does stress, however, is this: "Understanding can also go beyond the author's subjective act of meaning, and perhaps even necessarily and always goes beyond it" (p. 122).

Applied to the situation of social science interpretation, this clarification is well expressed by Ricoeur (1971): "Understanding has nothing to do with an *immediate* grasping of a foreign psychic life or with an *emotional* identification with a mental intention. Understanding is entirely *mediated* by the whole of explanatory procedures which precede and accompany it" (p. 561). The essentially dialectical workings of understanding, then, involve more than a particular "us" vis-à-vis a particular "them." In addition, both "we" and "they" are preconditioned by our respective traditions, specifically, by our assumptions, definitions, and criteria for determining what constitutes "truth" or "valid knowledge." Trying to disclose the other's world, to overcome cultural estrangement, without first recognizing the implications of one's own ontological world and epistemological premises, can only result in an artificially one-sided, naively nonreflective grasp of the situation. Indeed, Gadamer (1976) states that it is precisely this "authentic epistemological interest" that "distinguishes true sociologists from technicians of social structure" (p. 40).

When these ontological and epistemological issues *are* recognized, and when "understanding" is itself understood in the hermeneutic sense ("To understand a text is to follow its movement from sense to reference, from what it says, to what it talks about," says Ricoeur, 1971: 558), the way is opened for reflexive interpretation of social phenomena. Following Ricoeur's model, "meaningfully oriented behavior" (the "sense" of the text) and its "non-ostensive references" (its metasituational "reference") are *both* part of the ontological world we seek to grasp when attempting to understand the other. But while we as would-be interpreters may try in this way to overcome cultural estrangement, we are ourselves part of our own tradition's ontological world. Thus *our* attempts at making "sense" (engaging in the meaningfully oriented behavior of "research") and *our* meta- (non-ostensive) references to meanings beyond the immediate, in fact constitute the other half of the dialectic.

It is in this connection that Gadamer's concept of understanding as "a fusion of horizons" (a "horizon" for Gadamer implies a person's or a culture's preunderstandings, or "prejudices" in the nonpejorative, etymological sense of the term) is so relevant to reflective social science. Whether the two poles of the dialectic be we/they or the familiar/the alien, "collision with the other's horizons makes us aware of assumptions so deep-seated that they would otherwise remain unnoticed" (Linge, 1976: xxi).

Many anthropologists, at least informally, have uttered similar statements about their fieldwork experiences; perhaps more "natives" than we will ever know have likewise made similar remarks about their encounters with anthropologists. Whatever may be the case, such thoughts deserve more public consideration, particularly in the context of contemporary anthropologizing. Accordingly, Chapter 4, which brings together conclusions about the three questions introduced above, ends with some tentative reflections on "understanding" and interpretive methodology in the social sciences.

Chapter Two

The Transmission of Traditional Symbols through Formal Schooling

n the previous chapter I introduced the idea that two key symbols—the traditional image of the Dalai Lama and the newly emerging *rang-zen* metaphor and its annually dramatized scenario—both affect and are affected by Tibetans' ongoing attempts to make sense of their individual and social lives today. In this chapter I explore this idea in more detail, concentrating on the ways in which these symbols are deliberately as well as implicitly being transmitted to the young generation now attending Tibetan schools in India. At the same time, however, the effects of my own tradition's horizon can also be noted here, even, in fact, in the very way in which this chapter is organized.

Four different subtopics are considered here: the establishment of Tibetan schools in India; the explicit curriculum (including textbooks and subjects as well as pedagogical approaches and cocurricular activities); the implicit curriculum (values and attitudes); and the goals and implications of education in a Tibetan environment. The discussion that follows thus moves from a re-presentation of historical background to what Ricoeur would call "guessing" (as opposed to "validation"). It is furthermore a description, from my vantage point, of those sociocultural "facts" that I "saw," recorded, and ultimately tried to weave into a more comprehensive interpretation.

The various means by which all of this took place were likewise shaped not only by my previous academic training but by all of the other contingencies that had touched my life up to that time. At the beginning of my fieldwork, for example, I happily discovered that much of the basic information I was trying to get by an all-too-random casting about was already available in printed form, published by various Tibetan agencies and institutions. With a degree of relief that should be familiar to any former language and literature major, I set about reading and taking notes; the written verbal symbols were magically able to calm my fears about completing the all-important dissertation.

It would be far too simple and ultimately incorrect to say that I then progressed, in clear linear fashion, from reading, to "simple" interviewing and observing, to "complex" discussions and reflections about the ideas that ended up as my final conclusions. Yet some sort of processual movement most definitely was involved: an on-again, off-again spiral of self-perceived insight and ignorance, knowledge and naiveté. Some of this even found expression in that magical form, writing. Words and pages did multiply, and with them, the confidence to write like a symbolic anthropologist about the meanings and values I saw as most important to the Tibetans. Thus it came about that I, the apprehensive neophyte, began my study of *Tibetan* attempts to make sense of their situation!

As evidenced by their constant reference to this subject, these people are indeed deeply concerned about maintaining as much as they can of their cultural continuity. At the same time, however, they also realize that to survive as a group, they must adapt, especially economically and socially, to their present situation. For this reason, then, they regard the Tibetan school system, sponsored by the government of India, as critically important, for this institution not only serves to transmit traditional Tibetan knowledge but, by virtue of its modern, diversified curriculum, can potentially aid the young generation in their acculturation.

It is in this context, that is, in an environment that deliberately nourishes and strengthens the students' self-definition as modernizing Tibetans, that the symbol and the reality of the Dalai Lama is carefully and ubiquitously presented to Tibetan children. Other traditional cultural patterns are likewise emphasized here: knowledge of the Tibetan language and religion as well as cultivation of three primary Tibetan values and attitudes: *snying-rje* ("compassion"); *ya-rabs spyod-bzang* ("respectful behavior"); and *rgyal-zhen* ("patriotism," a recent version of the older virtue of ethnic or local-group pride). The symbol of the Dalai Lama, however, subsumes all of

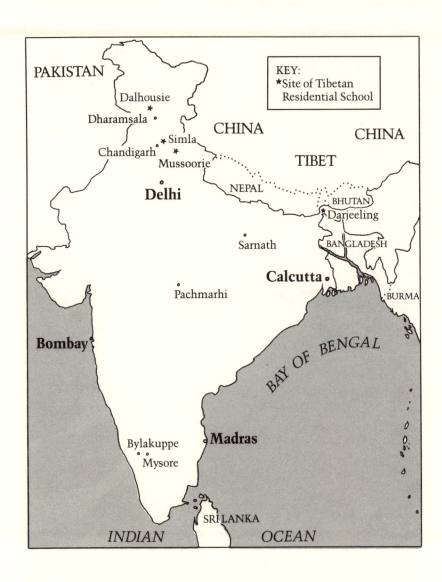

Map of India Showing Locations of Major
Tibetan Educational Institutions

these metaphors and paradigms. In the Tibetan school system, then, the Dalai Lama permeates the entire educational process, for in this capacity, as a summarizing symbol, he inspires commitment to the Tibetan ideological system as a whole.

The Establishment of Tibetan Schools in India

Less than a year after the abortive Lhasa uprising of March 1959, the first school for Tibetan refugee children was established by the Dalai Lama in Mussoorie, Uttar Pradesh (see map for locations of Tibetan schools). That such immediate priority be given to formal schooling at a time of such turmoil shows the degree to which education was regarded as a necessity and not a luxury by Tibetan leaders reacting to the loss of country and exile. The Dalai Lama (1962) himself stresses this point in his autobiography:

> It is even harder for children than for adults to be uprooted and taken suddenly to an entirely different environment. . . . We had to do something drastic to preserve their health—and their education was also a matter of great importance. We know that our children in Tibet are being snatched away from their parents and brought up as Chinese Communists, not as Tibetan Buddhists. . . . So, in the next generation, the children in India may be a very important people, a nucleus of the peaceful religious life which we wish to regain. p. 226)

This view of education as a means of keeping Tibetan culture alive among the young is uppermost in the minds of Tibetan policy makers today, but before investigating the goal itself, I should first explain the practical, if bureaucratic, bridge that had to be built to link the hopes and aims of these refugees with the pragmatic realities of life in their new host country.

Within a year after the opening of that first school in Mussoorie, the Council for Tibetan Education, an exclusively Tibetan office related to the government-in-exile, was established. Subsequently, two more schools, in Simla and in Darjeeling, were set up. By 1961 there were 800 Tibetan students enrolled in the three schools, and in May of that year, during the course of formal discussions between the Dalai Lama and Prime Minister Nehru regarding the rehabilitation of Tibetan refugees in India, a comprehensive educational program was mapped out. As a result of this meeting, an autonomous body ultimately under the jurisdiction of the government of India—the Central Committee on the Education of Tibetan Refugees—was set up by the Government of India Ministry of Education.

In September 1961 this committee became registered as a society whose purpose was to establish and administer schools for the children of Tibetan refugees. Newly renamed the Tibetan Schools Society, this organization could now administer existing and future Tibetan schools under the auspices of the Government of India Ministry of Education. Its governing body, composed of officials of the former Central Committee, included the union minister of education as ex-officio chairman and three representatives of the Indian government: a senior official of the Ministry of Education who was appointed full-time secretary of the society; a senior official from the Ministry of External Affairs, which at that time was responsible for the rehabilitation of Tibetan refugees in India; and the financial advisor to the Ministry of Education. In addition, three representatives of the Dalai Lama were also numbered among the governing body (*Tibetans in Exile: 1959–1969,* 1969: 226–227; *Tibetan Review,* 1968b: 8–9).

This brief description of the Tibetan Schools Society's initial organization is essentially applicable to the situation that persists today. Renamed (the second renaming) the Central Tibetan Schools Administration (CTSA) in 1969, this group is still directly related to the Indian government, with Indian ministerial representation comprising one-half of the membership of directors. In addition, the Union Ministry of Education still subsidizes the CTSA's budget; in 1968 this amounted to almost 98 percent of their total expenditures (*Tibetan Review,* 1968b: 11). Besides providing financial aid, the Ministry of Education has also made Indian educational expertise available to the Tibetan community in the person of administrators and teachers for the schools. Thus Tibetans sincerely and often express their gratitude to India for assisting in the establishment of schools that could potentially serve an entire younger generation. By 1977, more than 8,000 students had been or were being educated in this system, (*Tibetan Review,* 1977c: 7).

For the Tibetan community as a whole, then, this was the first time in their history that such educational opportunities were offered to so many, regardless of social class. For that very reason, in fact, the first Tibetan schools in India were hardly able to draw on the resources of their own people to staff and administer the institution. In addition to the acute financial problems suffered by the vast majority of the refugees, the group in general was quite unfamiliar with any kind of formal secular education beyond a narrow concentration on basic arithmetic, calligraphy, and memorization of the scriptures. There was an elite segment of the population from noble or nouveaux riches families who had been previously sent to India or other foreign countries to receive a modern education, but in no way did the sum of these individual experiences add up to a trained stock of native pedagogues. The first teachers and administrators, then, were overwhelmingly non-Tibetan, mostly Indians and occasionally foreigners such as airline stewardesses who would volunteer to teach English on a short-term basis.

This lack of a Tibetan teaching and administrative staff did not, however, lead to any radical change in the collective enculturation of the younger generation. Because so many parents were scattered in various parts of India working on road construction or were too destitute to provide adequately for their children's maintenance, let alone education, the first seven schools built by the Tibetan Schools Society (now the CTSA) were initially all residential institutions where the students lived in dormitories under the care of Tibetan guardians or houseparents. As for the day schools that were also set up, these were located in the Tibetan settlement camps established for large groups of Tibetans by the Indian government. Thus in both cases, the children were in close contact with Tibetan adults who, as real or surrogate parents, provided the primary nutriment, both in a literal sense and in terms of ethnic identity.

But the problem of professional staffing, which initially admitted of only one solution—non-Tibetans in positions requiring academic expertise—has been compounded by the fact that two decades have gone by since the school system was first set up. For one thing, the study of the Tibetan language is also an official part of the instructional program, and in this subject at least, the teachers could hardly be anything but Tibetan. In fact, the first language teachers were all monks, the traditional group in which intellectual specialists might be found. Despite the high degree of esteem traditionally accorded to learned monk scholars, however, the Council for Tibetan Education declared that even these individuals, "who had considerable knowledge in Tibetan studies . . . could not be entrusted with teaching the children in this new environment without being trained for it" (*Tibetans in Exile: 1959–1969*, 1969: 250).

Thus in March 1964, the Teachers Training Centre was started, with a Tibetan monk scholar as director and a Canadian teacher in charge of instructing the thirty trainees, all monks, in modern teaching methods, general knowledge, and English. The 1-year course was followed by a final examination given by the Council for Tibetan Education and the Council of Religious and Cultural Affairs, both of which are branches of the Tibetan government-in-exile. After the exam, the trainees were sent to visit three residential schools to gain practical teaching experience. The next year, the same program was repeated for a new group of 26 trainees, also monks, after which this particular program was terminated.[1]

This innovation thus gave the traditional category of Tibetan intellectual specialists, the monk scholars, first chance to receive the training that would enable them to continue their academic role in the new environment. Furthermore, its effect was to insure a supply of monk teachers in the Tibetan schools, an issue that is not entirely without controversy in the Tibetan community in India.

In considering some of the implications of this situation, it is well to relate it to the other educational development that is affecting the staffing of Tibetan schools. More and more young Tibetans are completing programs of higher study at Indian institutions, and many of these recent graduates are firmly committed to helping the Tibetan community by returning to teach in the Tibetan school system. This gradual but steady influx of qualified Tibetans into the CTSA system cannot but encourage the desire for more autonomy on the part of the Tibetan authorities, especially since the original reason for relying so heavily on Indian expertise—the lack of Tibetan know-how and resources—is becoming less and less applicable to the situation today. To illustrate these issues with some figures, at the time of my fieldwork, there were over 170 Tibetan teachers (in-

---

1. A similar teacher's training course for monks and laity alike is now offered through the facilities of the Institute of Higher Studies in Sarnath.

cluding monks) in the 4 residential and 29 day schools administered by the CTSA. The residential school at my fieldwork site had 38 teachers in all; of these, 28 were Indian, and of the remaining 10 Tibetans, 7 were lay and 3 were monk teachers.

Added to this is the general feeling among the Tibetan community, particularly those directly involved with education, that the present hierarchy, that is, the local school subordinated to the CTSA, which is in turn subordinated to the Government of India Ministry of Education, involves too much red tape. If these schools could instead be taken over completely by the Council for Tibetan Education, these people say, then the curriculum could more easily be modified to suit the particular needs of Tibetans living in India. Under the present set-up, for example, a course in traditional Tibetan art cannot be offered as a school subject because there is no prescribed syllabus already accepted by the whole bureaucratic chain for specifically *Tibetan* art. While this example does not represent a crucial issue in itself; it does illustrate the general problem from the Tibetan point of view: a multilayered bureaucracy ultimately subject to the Indian government cannot act with enough flexibility to be an efficient organization for a relatively small group of non-Indian refugees.

From two different directions, then, the growing number of trained, potential educators from within the Tibetan community—both monks and laity—has given rise to this same general concern, that the original patterns of organization and staffing in the Tibetan schools may no longer be adequate to serve the newest generation of students most effectively. Such criticism, whether directed against the institution of Tibetan monk teachers in the schools or against the continued predominance of Indian policies and numerical strength among administrators and teachers there, is raised cautiously rather than stridently in the Tibetan community, and it is by no means universally shared by all Tibetans. Nevertheless, the fact that people are criticizing what is, by their own admission, a critically important institution, is itself extremely significant. Indeed, from the perspective of philosophical hermeneutics, these instances of taking a stand, either for or against various aspects of this formal means of cultural transmission, very definitely involve reflective attempts at self-understanding.

With this in mind, then, let me briefly present some of the comments and criticisms being expressed by Tibetans about their school system. While paying attention to the content of these opinions, it is also important to note the form in which they occur: as editorials and letters to the editor appearing in a remarkably free and at times hard-hitting English-language monthly financed and edited in New Delhi exclusively by Tibetans.

One criticism leveled against some of the Indian teachers in the school system involves the issue of the English language itself, specifically, "English teachers who cannot pronounce their subject" (see *Tibetan Review*, 1976m). The problem of fluency or competence in this language is a complex one in India. Other English-medium schools (for Indian children) are likewise affected by all the social contingencies, attitudes, and implications that surround a mediator language bequeathed by a colonial past to a relatively new, poly-linguistic nation-state.[2] In the case of the Tibetan schools, however, the concern for "teachers who *really* know English" is particularly strengthened by Tibetans' conviction that fluency in this language is crucial for their economic and social upward mobility, all the more so because they are not citizens of this country. As they see it, too many of the Indian teachers in the Tibetan school system simply are not adequately qualified to each *in* English, let alone to teach English as a subject in its own right.

Another Tibetan criticism against some Indian teachers involves the latters' alleged lack of commitment to their work, with the occasionally added suggestion that perhaps this commitment should not even be expected of them in this situation, where "they are not teaching their own." In the words of one editorial,

> It is a fact that most of the teachers find themselves in [the Ti-betan] schools because they could not get [jobs] anywhere else, and perhaps this state of affairs should not surprise anyone in a developing country. It is the experience of every student from a Tibetan school that most of the *gurujis* (teachers) are either cramming for their degree exams or letter writing in class. It is not uncommon to find lady teachers knitting or gossiping in class. (*Tibetan Review*, 1976m: 4)

It should be pointed out that such criticisms seldom occur without qualification: the mention of Tibetan gratitude to the Indian

2. See Nowak (1978b: 51–54, 61–63) for a more complete discussion of this problem.

government for its support, a clarification that not *all* Indian teachers lack sincere interest in teaching Tibetan children, and even an attempt to link the act of criticizing with the positive consequences of living in a free country. Thus a follow-up editorial makes this statement: "If, however, the editor has taken too much liberty with an organization (CTSA) that has done much commendable work for the welfare of the Tibetan children, he apologizes. It is because the editor is educated and grown up in a democratic India" (*Tibetan Review*, 1976j: 3).

A third topic for criticism and countercriticism (also discussed in the two editorials) involves the Tibetan monk teachers in the schools. One side of the argument is basically this: Too many lama teachers, having spent their lives in monasteries, have a one-dimensional approach to life. If education is to involve more than the memorization of textbooks, then the teachers must be people who can take a multidimensional role in the schools, helping the students widen their horizons by means of cocurricular as well as classroom activities. While at least one lama teacher should remain in each school to teach the religious subjects, they should never predominate (numerically or in decision making) over qualified Tibetan lay teachers (*Tibetan Review*, 1976m: 4, 1976j: 4).

Response to the two editorials came in the form of 10 pages of letters to the editor, including a long countercriticism from an Indian principal who felt personally attacked by the general tone of the articles. In addition, a number of secondary and college students wrote in to amplify or challenge the editorials or to take issue with other letters. Those who defended present educational policies, particularly the institution of lama teachers, included a young official working for the Council for Tibetan Education, a student and the principal of the Buddhist School of Dialectics (a philosophy and logic college for monks), a former (Indian) headmaster of one of the Tibetan schools, as well as Tibetan students and former students themselves. Many letters elaborated this point made by a tenth-grade boy: irresponsible public criticism of revered Tibetan institutions can serve to "destroy the very root of our culture, religion, and tradition" (Wangyal, 1976).[3]

Also worth noting is the fact that one of the letters defending monk teachers came from an Indian, the former headmaster referred

3. See correspondence in *Tibetan Review* (1976g, 1976h).

to above: "I believe that every Tibetan school should have at least one or two lama teachers. Tibetan monks symbolize sacrifice and devotion with a considerable degree of purpose, which are essential elements of any useful and beautiful life for which a school should prepare the 'schooled'" (Khan, 1976: 21).

For both Tibetans and Indians, then, such letters and editorials represent a new vehicle of communication. Furthermore, the message of this communication testifies to the democratization that has been brought about by Indian education, whatever its imperfections. As long as they are functionally literate in English, both Tibetans and Indians can use this forum to express their opinions freely, forsaking the socially obligatory honorifics of their respective mother tongues. Thus the awkward phrases of an anonymous letter from a secondary school student are printed directly across the page from a verbose epistle cosigned by the Tibetan rector and the Indian principal of one of the residential schools. Neither the selection nor the layout of the correspondence shows any indication that criteria of age, rank, or education were used to determine which letters would be published, and where.

Yet, leaving aside the printed format and the language used, this new means of expressing divergent opinions is not without precedent in Tibetan history. Discussing the literary style of the archaic (pre-eleventh-century) Tibetan manuscripts found in the caves at Tun Huang, Stein (1972/1962) points out the significant role of proverbs and metaphors in these early texts: "Cunning, aptness, the art of telling truths or hinting at blame in a veiled and indirect way, play a great part in these compositions" (p. 255).

Ten centuries later, these same values apparently motivated more than one author of these letters to the editor. English maxims such as "Spare the rod and spoil the child" as well as translated Tibetan proverbs are both employed to bolster the weight of personal opinion. Thus a letter that protests public criticism of internal Tibetan problems quotes this bit of traditional wisdom to add further legitimacy to its author's point: "Do not tell the secrets of your heart even to your wife who has [borne you] three sons" (Lhakpa Tsering, 1976).

In the light of hermeneutic theory, this kind of interaction between familiar tradition and alien social environment is significant, for it reveals a high degree of personal involvement in the past—present dialectic of the current situation. Clearly, the Tibetan community identifies strongly with their schools in relation to their collective future. In fact, the specific changes these people would like to see in their educational system—more administrative independence from the Indian government, more Tibetan teachers in the classrooms, and better qualified teachers in general—reflect the very same attitude: "Our schools are our future."

Finally, any projected move in the direction of a totally autonomous Tibetan educational system, whatever its actual chances of materializing, can be seen as an ideal reversal of Tibetans' initial dependence on Indians for expertise. Such a wish is natural coming from a group that has already made considerable progress, both economically and educationally. Yet beyond this, the dual criticism of "poor teaching" and a low level of English competence, when leveled at Indian teachers by Tibetans, goes a step further than merely reversing the categories of the advisors and the advised. In a truly ironic confounding of medium and message, the critics have taken one of the topics of criticism and made it the language in which further criticisms are expressed! Viewed in this light, the letters to the editor are a fitting summary of all these issues, for not only do they require a certain degree of fluency in the literal sense, in English, but their very existence testifies to the fact that educated Tibetans are also achieving fluency in new codes of behavior: making critical evaluations of modern institutions effectively public. In short, the first Tibetan educatees have become the first educators, both inside and outside the classroom.

The Explicit Curriculum:
I. Textbooks and Subjects

The very notion of modern classroom instruction, complete with textbooks and a general course of studies, represents a radical departure from the traditional educational system in Tibet, where an emphasis on the written language, particularly its calligraphy, dominated all secular schooling.

At the primary stage the traditional system concentrated on teaching pupils to read and write the Tibetan language. At the next stage the scriptures were learnt by heart as they formed the main subject taught to monks and lay pupils in the Tibetan educational system. At a more advanced stage, limited only to monk scholars, the pupils took part in dialectical discussions with their teachers, and examinations at this level were also based on this pattern. Thus the educational system completely ignored scientific subjects, concentrating on the study of philosophy, and though such a system might have suited the needs of the people as it was then—isolated and unaware of the rest of the world—we feel it needs a thorough overhauling to suit the present situation. (*Tibetans in Exile*, 1969: 227–228)

From the very first year of exile, this conscious and officially endorsed desire to give "a thorough overhauling" to the traditional educational system has led Tibetans to look beyond their old horizons for new models of what education can imply.

The general principle followed in framing the educational system for these schools was that while due emphasis should be made in the teaching of Tibetan language, religion, and culture, the students should be given a thorough modern education so that the foundations could be laid for the training of future engineers, doctors, nurses, lawyers and other professions and technicians. Even in the teaching of traditional subjects such as Tibetan language and literature, efforts were made to incorporate modern methods. (*Tibetan Review*, 1968b: 9)

This flush of enthusiasm for modern subjects and methods is understandable, given such optimistic attraction to nontraditional professions, so it is not surprising that even the traditional areas of learning were affected by pedagogical innovations.

The primary example of this, the preparation of a series of textbooks that would gradually present instruction in Tibetan language, culture, history, and religion to school-going children, came as a result of a meeting called by the Dalai Lama in 1959. It is significant that the participants invited to this meeting included both religious and secular power holders: the members of the old Kashag (Tibetan cabinet), monk scholars from each of the four Buddhist sects, the Tibetan principal of the first (and only, at the time) Tibetan school, and two Tibetan lay scholars.

Although Tibetans had never before had textbooks as part of their traditional system of education, they were obviously not unaware of the potential this innovation would offer for the official presentation and spread of ideology. Not only could such a graded series of books be used to instruct the children about religion and traditional culture, but a systematic attempt could now be made to shape a more cohesive group identity among young Tibetans in exile.

One of the most divisive problems experienced by the Tibetan group as a whole has been regional factionalism, exacerbated by dialect differences and the proximity, while still in Tibet, to opposing geopolitical centers of influence, Lhasa or China in particular. A second source of mutual suspicion—sectarianism—was not nearly so operative in traditional Tibet as it has come to be in post-1959 refugee communities, for in the past, low population density and the remoteness of population centers made it possible for each of the four major sects to coexist without threatening the others' areas of influence. Now, however, with everyone in closer contact, differences in philosophical emphases and interpretations stand out more sharply; moreover, intersectarian awareness of the others' relative strength, in number as well as in influence, promotes a certain competitive attitude aggravated all the more by Western devotees seeking a very un-Tibetan "one true sect." In view of all this, concerned Tibetans from all sects, including the Dalai Lama himself, are engaged in a public relations campaign to stress harmony and unity among the sects. This is likewise true with respect to regional differences. The schools, by teaching the Lhasa (Central Tibetan) dialect as standard Tibetan for all refugees in exile, are consciously setting out to produce a more homogenous younger generation who are learning to put their national identity ahead of regional loyalties.

The following song, presented as the preface to the second-grade reader in the series of textbooks mentioned above, illustrates how deliberately the textbook planners sought to propagate the ideology of pan-Tibetanness. The lyrics begin by describing Tibet as a country at the top of the world surrounded by beautiful, snowy mountains, a land of great blue-green rivers and lakes, various wild animals, and precious natural resources. Then the geography is correlated with the three major regional identities: "In the east is Mdo-khams where the heroic Khampas live; in the north is Amdo, with its diligent Amdobas; in the center is Dbus-gtsang, the home of the religious Dbus-gtsang people." The final five lines of the song are particularly significant:

> yul de gsum-pa bod kyi yul
> mi-rigs de gsum bod rigs yin
> sha-rus gcig-pa sha-stag yin
> bod-mi yongs kyi spyi-nor du
> skyabs-mgon ta-la'i bla-ma bzhugs

> These three regions are Tibetan.
> These three types of people are Tibetan.
> We are only one race [literally, "flesh-and-bone"].
> The Universal Jewel for all Tibetan people
> Is the Protective Lord, the Dalai Lama.
> (*New Dawn Second Grade Textbook* [*'dzin-gra gnyis-pa'i slob-deb skya-rengs gsar-pa*], 1964: 1–2, my translation)

While acknowledging the three major regional groups and correlating each with its positive stereotype, the song ends with the quintessential summarizing symbol of Tibetanness, the Dalai Lama.

Besides stressing the ideology of a unified Tibetan nation, an identification that was never so true as it is now, the textbooks also serve as a means of informing the students about those aspects of their traditional culture that could not be transplanted to India. Thus sentences from the first-grade reader, besides including such universal standbys as "Each hand has five fingers" and "The balloons are red and yellow," also feature examples like "Milk comes from a *'dri* (the female of the yak species)" and "Yaks have two horns," referring of course to the most Tibetan of animals, which cannot survive in India and which most of the younger children have never seen.

Another function of these readers, which are obviously teaching much more than word recognition and spelling, might perhaps be characterized as easing the transition to a matter-of-fact familiarity with Western science. As is typical of primary texts in general, many of the sentences express simple observations about natural phenomena. A pair of phrases begins with the commonplace statement that "the shape of the moon is round" (*zla-ba'i dbyibs ni zlum-po red)*; but the next phrase is more significant: "According to Western science, the moon does not have its own light; the light of the sun falls on it" *(phyi'i tshan-rig ltar-na zla-ba rang la 'od yod-pa ma red / zla-ba la nyi-ma 'od phog gi yod-pa red)*. Such a presentation neither denies nor exalts Western science; it simply treats it as one point of view and leaves open the implication that there might be others.

This openness to multiple epistemologies supports traditional definitions of *knowledge* too. For homework one night, the second-grade class (ages ranging from about 6 to 10) had to memorize the 12-year cycle of astrological animals, and the next day those who could not recite the sequence in proper order were publicly chastized by having chalk zeros (the word *zero* was said in English) drawn on their foreheads. This incident well illustrates the point made to me by a Tibetan rector regarding these language classes:

> Although our curriculum follows that of the Central Schools Organization [referring to the schools established throughout India for the Indian children of Central Government employees], there are certain modifications with respect to the teaching of language. For us, Tibetan is not just a second lanuage, as is the case [with Hindi or English] in other schools; it includes a strong emphasis on Tibetan culture as well.

Thus the language classes serve as a particular means of transmitting traditional culture, while the original goal of providing students with "a thorough modern education" continues to motivate general educational policy. In line with that aim, the Tibetan schools have adopted a common syllabus for grades 1 through 8, with standardized curricula, courses, and textbooks all prepared by the National Council of Educational Research and Training. Besides the three languages (English as the general medium of instruction, Hindi as the national language, and Tibetan), other subjects taught include mathematics, science, social studies, physical education, art, and music. The schools having grades 9 and above are affiliated with the Central Board of Secondary Education, and their programs of studies are likewise standardized, particularly with a view toward preparing students for the All-India Higher Secondary Examination.

This exam, given every year in March at the completion of secondary school studies, serves as a nationally recognized measure of academic achievement. It is administered over a period of approximately 2 weeks and consists of separate tests covering each subject studied. The raw scores are totaled and the results, made public in July, are used as criteria for admission to Indian institutions of higher study. Before 1976 the exams were given at the end of the eleventh grade; since then, however, there has been a significant change in policy, reflecting the Indian government's attempts to deal with the widespread problem of "the useless B.A.s and the educated unemployed."

To counter the prevailing notion that a college education will automatically improve one's economic and social status, a new scheme, the 10 + 2 system, has been inaugurated. According to this plan, all tenth graders in India take a set of comprehensive exams at the end of that year of study. Unlike the previous scheme, which classed results as "pass" (with the individuals then ranked into divisions) or "fail," the exams taken after grade 10 will not terminate anyone's school career. What they will do, however, is determine the basic orientation of each student's final 2 years of secondary school: the higher scorers will follow a more specifically precollege program, and the others will be tracked into vocational training.

While the theory behind the 10 + 2 system finds ready acceptance by all who are concerned about the economic relevance and quality of postsecondary education in India, the practical realities of implementing the plan are another matter. As the new policy only went into effect in 1976, the first examinations of this type were not given until March 1977. The issue was thus very topical while I was in India. Indian newspapers, particularly the editorial pages and letters to the editor, were full of opinions on the subject. The objections raised against this new system stemmed basically from two sorts of problems associated with its implementation: the lack of funding and facilities for this new emphasis on vocational training, and the traditional disdain for manual labor, which cripples any attempt to encourage vocational diversification.

The scope of the first problem can be better understood by considering that even in Delhi, not to mention the rural areas, less than 50 percent of the schools were estimated, at the time of my fieldwork, to have had the specialized teachers and equipment necessary for putting the new program into practice. In this respect, the much smaller Tibetan school system had a great advantage over its Indian counterpart, where it was feared that any shift in emphasis toward vocational training would draw scarce resources away from the standard curriculum, which could ill afford any such depletion. Tibetans, however, already had their own vocational training institute at Pachmarhi, central India, which was opened in 1965 to provide training for the teenagers and young adults who had never been to school before and who would have been very much overage in regular classrooms. This institute, staffed by Tibetans who had recently received specialized mechanical training abroad, can now provide the final 2 years of vocational instruction in carpentry, welding, machine operation, masonry, and tailoring for Tibetan students desirous of or tracked into such a program.

The other problem associated with the 10 + 2 system—negative attitudes toward manual labor—applies to both Indian and Tibetan societies, although the Tibetan case is less complicated by deep-seated identifications of occupation, caste, and related associations of purity or pollution. Nevertheless, the aspirations of most Tibetan secondary students have tended toward a vague and idealized attraction to professional or desk-job careers, that is, toward becoming a teacher, nurse, secretary, or clerk in a Tibetan government office. As pointed out in a *Tibetan Review* editorial:

> Being the first Tibetan generation undergoing the process of "modernisation," the Tibetan youth does not have the advantage of parental guidance in selecting a career suitable to his ability and interest. As a result he makes a haphazard decision, often based on out-moded notions and finds himself in confusion after the long-awaited graduation. A favourite subject, for instance, among the more successful Tibetan school leavers is English, with the traditional ambition of becoming a "secretary," whose connotation in Tibetan language seems even more irresistible.[4] Unless there is a fundamental change of attitude which will free them from this white-collarism, Tibetan graduates with their vague general courses are likely to find them-

4. In Tibetan, the word *drung-yig* suggests a civil officer, usually of official government rank. Furthermore, the title "secretary" is used all over India to refer to the head or chief official of an organization. Thus there are actually three possible connotations suggested by the English word *secretary*: a high official, a low-level bureaucratic functionary, and an office worker-cum-typist.

selves in the long queue of "educated unemployed." (*Tibetan Review*, 1973c: 3, 11)

This editorial was written barely 13 years after the first official attempts were made to give a thorough overhauling to the traditional system of education, and it testifies to the somewhat ironic success of the new policies and innovations. By replacing the old, narrow concentration on language instruction with a modern curriculum covering many subjects, the Tibetan school system is indeed producing graduates who can go on to complete their education at institutions of higher learning. Yet these same students, with their expectations of the good life raised and complicated by their modern education, are now subject to the confused disillusionment that all too often follows when such expectations cannot be met.

The Explicit Curriculum: II. Pedagogical Approaches and Cocurricular Activities

While new textbooks and a more general course of subjects both represent modern innovations involving major changes from the traditional curriculum, pedagogical approaches, particularly the methods used in the Tibetan language classes, have retained much of their original character. An important example may be seen in the way reading, writing, and spelling is taught to young children.

The Tibetan dialect spoken in all the schools, Modern Central Tibetan, is that of Dbus province, where Lhasa, the capital, is located. The phonetic structure of this dialect, which is now spoken or at least understood by nearly all Tibetans living in India, has evolved considerably from that which probably prevailed in the seventh and eighth centuries, when the writing system was codified. For this reason, the pronunciation of Modern Central Tibetan often differs greatly from what the orthography would suggest. For example, the perfective form of the verb that means "to attain, accomplish" is spelled *bsgrubs* but pronounced ṭu.[5] The word for *north*, spelled

5. See M. Goldstein's dictionary (1975a: 24) for the phonetic values of the transcription used here.

byang, is pronounced chaŋ; and the word for *opinion* spelled *bsam-'char,* is pronounced sāmcaa.

In addition, active, and not just passive, knowledge of the written language requires a further consideration: the orthography must not only be known, but in writing, it must also be arranged properly. Syllables in written Tibetan are composed of a possible combination of one to six consonants and one vowel. The way of writing the letters, however, is not completely linear; nonsyllabic (i.e., consonantal) "prefixes," superscripts, and subjoined consonants may also occur. The following scheme shows the order in which the letters are read; it is this progression that is followed when Tibetan orthography is transcribed into roman script.

$$(V)$$
$$C^2$$
$$C^1 + C^3 + C^5 + C^6$$
$$C^4$$
$$(V)$$

There are constraints on the consonants that can occur in each of the optional C^1, C^2, C^4, C^5, and C^6 positions. The C^3 slot, which *must* be filled, can be occupied by any consonant. The vowel, if it is not an unwritten *a,* which would be inherent in C^3, will either occur below C^4 (if it is a *u*), or above C^2 or C^3 (if it is an *i, e,* or *o*); in any case, it is read *after* C^3 even if it is positioned above it. To summarize with some examples:

$$
\begin{array}{l}
C^2 \\
C^3
\end{array}
\quad = \quad
\text{ལྷ}
\quad = \quad
\begin{array}{l}
l \\
h(a)
\end{array}
= \text{lha}
$$

$$
\begin{array}{l}
(V) \\
C^3 + C^5 \\
C^4
\end{array}
\quad = \quad
\text{གློག}
\quad = \quad
\begin{array}{l}
o \\
gg \\
l
\end{array}
= \text{glog}
$$

$$
\begin{array}{l}
C^2 \\
C^1 + C^3 + C^5 + C^6 \\
C^4 \\
(V)
\end{array}
\quad = \quad
\text{བསྒྲུབས}
\quad = \quad
\begin{array}{l}
s \\
bgbs \\
r \\
u
\end{array}
= \text{bsgrubs}
$$

When Tibetan children learn to read and write, they begin with simple syllables, starting with the letters of the alphabet (C^3, with all the vowel combinations), progressing to words with consonant finals (C^5 and C^6), gradually learning words with superscripts (C^2) and subscripts (C^4). Not until all these combinations have been taught will the C^1 "prefixes" be introduced, and only after much practice will complex words such as *bsgrubs* be presented.

The method of teaching this complicated orthography is unique. From the very earliest days of primary school, the spellings are sung, or more correctly, chanted, to a tune that incorporates all the implicit rules of phonetic realization. As the names of the letters are chanted in progression, the morpheme *btags* [tāà] ("to attach, affix"; allomorph [ptāà]) is inserted after the consonant combinations involving C^2 or C^4. This has the effect of creating "subtotals" of letter combinations, so that, for example, the syllable written as *spyan* (honorific for "eye") will be phonetically realized according to the following process, which involves pronouncing all nine syllables (i.e., naming the letters, twice indicating the "subtotals," and twice including the morpheme *btags* [tāà]), ultimately ending with the proper phonetic pronunciation, cēēn.

ষ ্	ষ্	
s + *p* +"attached"	→ *spa*	→
[sā] + [pāp] +[tāà]	→ [pā] (first "subtotal")	
্	ষ্	
+ *y* +"attached"	→ *spya*	→
[yā] +[tāà]	→ [cā] (second "subtotal")	
ৰ	ষ্ৰ·	
+*n*	→ *spyan*	
+[na]	→ [cēēn] (final pronunciation)	

Other syllables can also be part of the chanted formula, as for example, [wɔ], which follows C^1 when that consonant occurs, and the names of the four alphabetically distinct vowels, which are all bisyllabic and pronounced quite differently from the sounds they represent:

schools are definitely succeeding in imparting a passive knowledge of the written language. Graduates of these schools are universally literate, at least in terms of being able to read and copy. Even small children, presented with a written word whose meaning is completely unfamiliar to them, can unhesitatingly crack the complicated orthographic code and arrive at the proper pronunciation.

But the ability to create and compose, which in Tibet used to be emphasized in the form of elaborate letter-writing practice, now suffers by comparison when forms—in this case, the letters of the alphabet—are given so much more attention than content. Although my own ability to read handwritten Tibetan hardly qualified me to judge the performance of older students in this respect, I often noted how friends of mine, educated trilingual Tibetans in their 20s, would usually write letters to each other in English rather than in Tibetan. The common, though by no means exclusive, preference for English by this age group of course involves other factors, considered in the next chapter. Nevertheless, the universal response to my questioning of the use of written English to friends who would be spoken to in Tibetan was this" "We don't always know the spelling. It would be embarrassing to make mistakes in writing, and English is so much easier."

Such an explanation is instructive on several counts. First, the evaluation of English as the "easier" written language has more behind it than the relative complexity of Tibetan orthography. As a foreign language, neither taught nor learned by native speakers, English is not likely to be invested with the extralinguistic emotional significance characteristic of a native language taught by and to native speakers living in exile. Thus expectations of what constitutes proper performance in English tend to stop at the correct realization of explicit grammatical rules. Tibetan, however, is not just *a* language; it is *the* language of being Tibetan.

The amount of emphasis language classes put on the perfect reproduction and recognition of written forms may be judged excessive by non-Tibetans, but such an evaluation is likely influenced by criteria based on the Western equation of creativity with originality and uniqueness. Other aspects of Tibetan culture, notably the canons of Tibetan iconography, show a similar preoccupation with studied sameness of form, an emphasis that does not deny creativity but shifts its locus to the unobservable realm of meditation. In such a context:

The production of the work can in itself be an exercise in meditation; in this case the artist must make himself so familiar with the object he is producing that he brings it forth entirely from his own self, and yet he must do this in such a way that not only does a universally valid specimen emerge but each detail can be ritually justified; otherwise the result cannot serve the desired end. In this way the production of works of art is completely committed. Any freedom in the creation of form would signify imprecision, which would make the object invalid for its intended function and which would have rather a disturbing than an inspiring effect as soon as the object were used for purposes of meditation. (Pott, 1968: 155)

All this is not meant to imply that simple sentences written in Tibetan are subject to the same restrictions and expectations as the whole complex realm of Tibetan iconography. The uses of art and writing in Tibet have never coincided exactly, despite certain similarities in their regard for the precise reproduction of form. Still, it is important to point out that both script and scriptures have been treated with religious respect in this culture ever since the seventh century, when the Tibetan king Srong-btsan sgam-po sent his minister Thon-mi Sambhota to India to devise an alphabet that could be used to write the Tibetan language. According to a fifteenth-century historical work:

In the beginning of the Doctrine, in the reign of Tho-tho-ri gnyan-btsan, though religious books had become available (in Tibet), there was no one to write, read or explain (their meaning). In the reign of Srong-btsan sgam-po, Thon-mi Sam-bhota was sent to India. He thoroughly studied the alphabet and the (Sanskrit) language with the acarya Devavitshima (Lha'i rig-pa seng-ge). On his return to Tibet, he created the thirty letters of the Tibetan alphabet from the fifty letters of the Indian (alphabet). . . .

He then first taught the (new) script to the king. After that he taught it to some of the (king's) subjects known for their intelligence, and the (script) spread over the greater part of Tibet, and all were fortunate to perceive the Teaching of the Blessed One. (Roerich, 1976: 39, 219)

Writing in Tibet has had its mundane, secular uses, too, but the near worship of perfect form, as evidenced by the extreme emphasis given traditionally to calligraphy, probably owes much to this long association of written word and sacred, symbolic vehicle. Given such an attitude, it indeed seems likely that the fear of making mistakes in writing would weigh more heavily in this culture than in a situation in which writing is regarded merely as an efficient, pragmatic invention.

The explanation that it would be embarrassing to make mistakes also illustrates another aspect of the pedagogical approaches used in the Tibetan schools. As in traditional Tibet, but to a less extreme degree, the primary means of appealing for good behavior (including both academic diligence and respectful obedience) involves the use of shame sanctions. Sensitivity to *ngo-tsha* ("shame, embarrassment"; literally, "hot face") is highly developed in this society, and the concomitant notion of "face" receives an equally significant emphasis in the socialization process. Through their own experiences of being chastized, and also by observing the reactions of others, children learn that humiliation can be far more ego-threatening than actual physical pain. This culturally shared expectation underlies the disciplinary approach taken by Tibetan educators, both traditional and modern. Even though the severity of such measures is now much less, a certain continuity exists in the type of discipline administered in Tibetan schools, past and present: a combination of ridicule and corporal punishment.

In the traditional setting, as exemplified here by a pre-Chinese school in Lhasa, exams were held twice a month, with the grading based solely on the students' handwriting. According to a Tibetan woman who attended this school as a child:

> All the tests on paper are given to the Headmaster for final decision, after which the Headmaster distributes the papers, calling out loud the student's name and rank. As each name is called the student stands and takes his place according to his rank. When all the students in one class have been called and are lined up, the student in first place is given the bamboo and he hits all those who are below him. Then the second one does the same and so on until the last. The last one has to hit

an empty yak-skin bag three times and prostrate three times. After this the rest of the students will shout ridicule. In addition, he is told to sing, or dance, or bark like a dog, etc. Then the next class group goes through the same ritual. (C. Goldstein, n.d.: 11)

In this case, the worst punishment of all, reserved only for the lowest scoring student, is not the beating, which all but the top student would share, but the humiliation of being made to look ridiculous in everyone else's eyes. The beating or slapping that occurred in the traditional schools, painful as it might have been in purely physical terms, apparently left few if any scars on one's psyche, for:

Corporal punishment was considered the only effective means of disciplining a naughty boy. We feared our teacher, not because he was a tyrant, but because he was our guru; so we respected him and loved him as well. When I escaped to India and went to school in Kalimpong, I was surprised at the resentful manner in which the students took even a gentle admonition from their teachers. Small as we were in Saskya, we took every thrashing from the teacher as an act of kindness, and never felt hurt mentally. We consoled ourselves with the thought that, because the teacher cared for us, he took pains to thrash us for the sake of discipline. In Kalimpong I found this attitude was quite beyond the comprehension of Westernized students. (Dawa Norbu, 1974: 122)

In the Tibetan schools today, the older attitude of not sparing the rod has given way to a much more moderate use of physical force, especially on the part of the younger Tibetan teachers; nevertheless, secondary students still fear the occasional lama teacher who does not hesitate to crack down hard on the knuckles of an inattentive or lazy pupil. Furthermore, some vestiges of the liberal use of corporal punishment remain, even at the primary school level. In the school where I observed, for example, the traditional role of *rgan-bdag* [qɛn taà] (a type of teacher's assistant, translated for me by Tibetan teachers as "monitor") is still filled by an older, bigger student, who is responsible for the general order and diligence of the class while the teacher is busy checking individual work. As symbols of their authority, the *rgan-bdag* carry switches about 2 feet long and ½ inch thick, which they do not hesitate to use if they deem it necessary. One day, while the teacher was occupied in another part of the room, children began getting out of their seats and walking sociably around the classroom. The *rgan-bdag* proceeded to crack these errant souls over the head, hitting one little boy so hard that he was at first too stunned to react, after which he fought tears, went back to his seat, and there cried silently for about 2 minutes. The incident drew very little attention, and no one, teacher and victim included, appeared to question the justice of it.

But in general, the use of corporal punishment as a disciplinary measure is much less common now than it was in the past. There are no longer any floggings, nor are pupils subject to the old practice of *snyug-lcab* [ñūq ca]: having a piece of bamboo snapped against the palm (for girls) or the cheek, which has first been puffed out with air so that the flesh will not be cut (*snyug-lcab* on the cheek was only done to boys because it was feared that hitting girls on the face would spoil their beauty). In fact the incident I described above is the only case I ever saw of a child being struck to the point of tears, and even this was done not by the teacher but by a student "monitor" who seemed to be carried away by his role.

Much more than any form of corporal punishment, the use of shame sanctions serves as a means of correcting misbehavior in the schools today. When I first started to observe in the primary school, before I had become a more or less standard fixture, sharing a desk with another student in the back row, my presence initially served to give added force to the teacher's reprimand, which became "*Ngo-tsha! Phyi-rgyal der 'dug!*" ("Shame! There's a foreigner here!"). The latter part of the admonition was soon dropped, but "*Ngo-tsha!*" continued to be used whenever a pupil was disruptively inattentive or when anyone's work fell below acceptable standards.

Besides this very common, ordinary type of shaming, other means were also used to draw unfavorable attention to students who deserved it in the teacher's estimation. I have already mentioned the children who could not recite the 12-year cycle of astrological animals correctly; these *ma-shes-pa* ("ones who do now know") had chalk zeros drawn on their foreheads and were made to stand up while the "knowledgeable ones" recited the information from their seats. In another case, when corrected tests (sentences copied off the board) were handed back to the second-grade class, the ones who failed—eight boys and three girls—were lined up at the board facing their classmates. The teacher admonished them by saying "*Ngotsha!*" several times; then he invited the children at their seats to laugh at them. After this, the mistakes were pointed out, and the individuals were gently, even humorously chided. While 10 of the children thus shamed appeared none too crushed by the experience, at times even snickering along with the others, one girl reacted with a much stronger consciousness of "face"; during the entire chastisement she refused to look at the teacher or the class, all the while averting her eyes and "facing" away from others, toward the blackboard.[7]

The most elaborately staged manipulation of shame sanctions, however, occurred not in the classroom but outside, in the presence of all the teachers, school administrators, and the entire student body. This event, called "Proclamations," took place on the last day of the school year. Officials sat on a raised dais, and students, specially dressed in their identical, school-issue *phyu-ba* [chūpə] (Tibetan native dress), sat cross-legged on mats in the school courtyard below. Each homeroom teacher read out the names and final marks of every student in his or her class, along with the ultimate result: pass (in all subjects), promotion (passed on the average of all the subjects), special promotion (due to illness or other extenuating circumstances), or fail. As each name was read out, the individual had to rise, a shaking, solitary figure standing above a sea of hundreds of seated fellow students. Never was the etymology of the word *ngotsha* more apt. Pupils instinctively covered their "hot faces" with their hands, and those who were especially shamed by failure tended to bend almost double to avoid facing the gaze of others.

As for other, less outstanding examples of the pedagogical approaches used in the Tibetan schools, these can be briefly characterized as typical of almost all nonprivate schools in India: a strong emphasis on the memorization of textbooks and a laissez faire attitude toward active participation by the students. According to young Tibetan teachers who were themselves students in the Tibetan schools, the more creative, evocative pedagogy takes place in the primary schools, where the all-Tibetan staff, some of whom

7. This kind of learned reaction to public shaming can have adverse effects on Tibetans' self-confidence later in their educational careers, if they go on to attend modern colleges and universities (see Nowak, 1978a: 196).

have had Montessori training, tries harder to stimulate interest and active student participation. Though I was never able personally to compare the two classroom situations (government-sponsored school and private funded primary school), my observations of the younger students tended to support the judgment of the Tibetan teachers. The primary school children I saw participated with great zest, and also volume, in group activities such as spelling, reciting times tables, or singing. In addition, as individuals they vied with one another to lead the class in the recitation of the alphabet and the spelling of words on the board; as a whole, they walked to school expectant and happy, particularly after a vacation.

The final aspect of the explicit curriculum I consider here— cocurricular and free-time activities—includes compulsory and optional projects directly organized by the schools as well as pastimes students can select during their leisure hours. The first of these, religious instruction, must take place outside the regular school curriculum, as government-supported schools in India are not allowed to teach any particular religion as part of their official academic program. For this reason, then, the rector of each residential school organizes a weekly, compulsory evening class for the older students. There, the rectors or one of the monk teachers gives explanatory talks on Buddhism, Tibetan culture, and Tibetan history, particularly modern Tibet-China relations.

In addition, on every religious holiday, the senior monk teacher gives a sermon explaining its meaning and its traditional celebration. (Such explanations are given because many Tibetan holidays are now celebrated in very abbreviated fashion owing to Tibetans' situations as refugees. In a host country, they feel that less time can be taken off from work to engage in what formerly would have been week-long festivities.) The students also attend ½-hour prayer sessions twice a day, in the morning after out-door calisthenics and in the evening before supper. Finally, there are occasions when the whole school community—students, Tibetan teachers, and dormitory houseparents—all take part in special prayer and incense-burning ceremonies (*bsangs-gsol*) at the summit of the prayer hill located behind the school. Such occasions commonly occur as part of the celebration of Buddhist holy days, but one such instance I observed was marked by more than the usual blend of religious supplication and political awareness: a special *bsangs* ceremony held immediately after Mao's death. Official Chinese accusations against the Gang of Four and a radical shift in official Chinese attitude toward Deng Xiaoping were viewed by many Tibetans as hopeful signs that internal problems in China might lead to an amelioration of the situation in Tibet.

A second cocurricular activity, described to me by a Tibetan college student as "a significant democratic innovation," is the student council that exists at the school I studied. Established by the school's first Tibetan principal, an older man familiar with both Western institutions and traditional Tibetan government, this organization gives students their first experience with elected representation. At the head of the student council is the school captain, considered a thoroughly responsible person by students and teachers alike. Besides taking the chief leadership role in the student activities that require it (organizing volunteer work crews, for example), this person will occasionally act as the spokesperson for the entire student body at such functions as the "Proclamations" or the school-leaving ceremonies. Under the school captain are four school prefects, elected from among the group leaders, who are themselves in charge of from 10 to 15 students each. The school captain and prefects are allowed to sit in on the monthly faculty meetings that involve all the Tibetan staff—rector, Tibetan teachers, and houseparents—and are free to bring up any points at this time. The elected group leaders and their groups, each presided over by one Tibetan teacher, have weekly meetings where the same principle is in effect. Any complaints, grievances, ideas, or problems can be brought up at these sessions, and if administrative action seems warranted, the matter will be officially conveyed to the rector or the principal.

Besides these two spheres of activity, one mainly religious, the other a kind of initiatory democratic experience, there are additional opportunities for student participation. A dance and drama club enables interested students to learn traditional songs, instrumental folk music, and dances from Tibetan experts in these areas. Sports, particularly basketball and soccer, are very popular among the boys especially, and other more specialized extracurriculars such as the school newspaper, woodcraft, or sewing classes can also be elected. In addition, each student is expected to spend ½ hour a day doing manual labor, which usually involves keeping the premises clean or, in the rainy season, growing vegetables for the school kitchen. Every now and then this requirement is challenged by a student who would rather eschew such grass-roots egalitarianism. The student always loses, however, for this policy represents a deliberate and well-enforced attempt on the part of the schools to eradicate any idle-rich pretensions or simple disdain for manual labor. Such attitudes, if allowed to persist on a large scale, would be disastrous for the Tibetan community in exile, which can ill afford to fracture into occupational castes. The compulsory work experience thus serves as both a leveling device and a shaper of attitudes: students' tasks are rotated so they can learn how to do everything, and anyone who tries to protest by alluding to an aristocratic family past is promptly told that those days are gone forever.

Finally, one last sphere of activity merits notice, even though it is neither organized by the schools nor an official part of any curriculum. In their leisure time—that is, in the after-school hours before evening prayers, on Sundays, and on holidays—the students at these schools are usually engaged in none of the activities I have described. Free time is of course spent enjoying some of the universal pastimes of children everywhere: games, un- or disorganized athletic competition, walks with friends, trips to the corner shop to buy, or gaze longingly at, the local equivalent of penny candy, and so on. But in addition, these students, fluent in Hindi and no strangers to the ubiquitous outpourings of Indian pop culture, are also becoming part of the global village, particularly in its more neon-lit, acoustically amplified aspects. Movie magazines, transistorized film music, a small but constantly used record collection, and special-occasion trips to the cinema halls in town all provide material for fantasy and escape, much to the consternation of the monk teachers and the older houseparents, who are frankly disturbed when they perceive students making heroes and heroines out of film stars and pop singers.

But like all fantasies, this idolization of the stylish and the celebrated does not last forever, nor is it as entirely directionless as some would fear. During my stay in India, perhaps the most popular rock hit of all, played repeatedly at any gathering of Tibetan teenagers and young adults, was the Carl Douglas song "Kungfu Fighting." The lyrics, extolling fast and funky Oriental martial skill, seem to have a powerful attraction for the older Tibetan boys especially. The image portrayed by this song, like that portrayed by the idolized late actor

Bruce Lee, speaks directly to the concern these young people have for tough, courageous models who do *not* lose their native turf to a bigger aggressor. Another popular song, which many of the older students have copied into their songbooks, is the Woody Guthrie paean to American manifest destiny "This Land Is Your Land." The lyrics, which have been changed to describe Tibetan geography and customs (in English), reveal a similar orientation in these young people's search for particularly significant themes and heroes: each verse concludes with the statement "This land belongs to you and me."

In concluding my considerations of the explicit curriculum—the textbooks, subjects, pedagogical approaches, and cocurricular activities used or offered by these schools—let me briefly highlight some of the continuities and discontinuities implied by the present educational system. Textbooks specifically designed for mass instruction never existed in old Tibet, and their use in all classes, Tibetan as well as general subjects, does constitute an innovation. Yet the Tibetan scholars and officials who prepared the modern Tibetan readers were evidently not unfamiliar with the potential offered by such learning tools, not only as a graded method of presenting factual information but as a systematic means of incorporating ideology—in this case, the cultural and political ideal of pan-Tibetan unity—into textual material. In fact, a very similar attitude has marked the tradition of more than 10 centuries of Tibetan historical literature: "The historical works themselves were not infrequently written with the undisguised intention of promoting the greater glorification and spread of the Buddhist religion" (Vostrikov, 1962: 49, my translation). Thus the present use of textbooks, a new institution, actually involves an old strategy: spreading official doctrine via committed, doubly "instructive" written works.

As for the wide variety of subjects now taught in the schools, Tibetans themselves have recognized a need to "modernize our education with the introduction of scientific subjects and humanities" (*Tibetans in Exile*, 1969: 228). This shift in emphasis from a specialized concentration on calligraphy and reading to a diversified curriculum that values Western science is, of course, unprecedented; but again, the strategy behind this move is not. In the past, Tibet may have been isolated by geography and attitudes, but when she truly desired to adopt something from beyond her borders, as is most notably exemplified by her interest in Buddhism, "no effort or cost seemed too much." In fact, "there is an extraordinary pragmatism in their approach to new things (if they decide to approach them at all), which might seem to be completely at variance with the mystical and philosophical preoccupations of their religious life" (Snellgrove and Richardson, 1968: 236). Just as, centuries ago, the teachings, translators, scholars, and even a writing system associated with Buddhism were all eagerly sought as desiderata to be attained without fail, a similar goal-directedness exists today with respect to the economic and social welfare of the Tibetan community. For this purpose, a general education is deemed indispensable, and the new, diversified curriculum this implies has been adopted pragmatically and energetically as the obvious means to that end.

Pedagogical approaches used in the schools show perhaps the least degree of change from their traditional form. Reading is still taught in the unique, time-honored manner, and the use of shame sanctions as a disciplinary measure continues to be a part of formal as well as informal educational practice. But despite some continuity in the emphasis given to the passive aspects of knowing the written language, there has been a marked decrease in the emphasis given to calligraphy. This change is again pragmatically motivated, for elegant handwriting alone can hardly be considered adequate preparation for informed participation in today's world. In the case of the shame sanctions, however, the continued cultivation of a sensitivity to "face" seems to indicate that this aspect of a collective and individual Tibetan self-image comes much closer to being a core value than, for example, beautiful calligraphy or a single-minded academic focus on religious texts.

Finally, the cocurricular activities offered in the schools should be regarded with special attention, for they involve the greatest amount of choice on the part of the students. Obligatory participation in religious functions, student government, and work brigades still leaves other areas such as sports, music and dance, and popular media to be selected on the basis of individual interest. In all these cases, it is significant that clear-cut boundaries between areas tend to blur. Religion and politics, for example, co-occur in worship services that directly refer to the contemporary status of Tibet, and young people's search for relevant themes and heroes brings their "Tibetanness" face to face with nontraditional pop culture. In short, these cocurricular activities, like the other aspects of the explicit curriculum, serve as powerful transmitters of both old and new forces affecting ethnic self-definition.

The Implicit Curriculum: Values and Attitudes

In these as in any schools, the explicit program represents only a part of what is being taught and learned. Given the express concern of the Dalai Lama and his government for preserving and fostering a strongly Tibetan Buddhist ideology among the school-going generation, it is particularly instructive to examine the self-definition so often stated by these students: *"Nga bod-pa yin"* ("I am Tibetan").[8]

During the winter vacation, when I was helping tenth- and eleventh-grade students review for the English section of the all-India exam, I had a good opportunity to ask for written responses to open-ended questions. In the course of assigning these "practice" compositions, I asked the eleventh-grade students one question that had nothing to do with the upcoming exam and everything to do with my fieldwork: "What do you mean when you say 'I am a Tibetan'?" I explained this to students in both English and Tibetan, adding that in this case I would not be concerned with English grammar or spelling, that their written responses would be helping me in my research, and that if they preferred, they could answer in Tibetan rather than in English. (Only three students did so, probably because the majority of the class still considered my request in the context of an English class.) The following responses, while more elaborate and articulate than the rest, are nonetheless representative of all the fifteen answers I received. I have made only minor changes (tense and article use) to smooth out the Engish.

8. The term *bod-pa* ("Tibetan") requires some clarification, as its reference has only recently been extended to include Tibetans from outside central Tibet. As M. Goldstein points, out, "Actually, this term, even in 1959, was used by Eastern Tibetans to refer only to Central Tibetans. They considered themselves *khams-pa* rather than *bod-pa*, and many of them actively sought to remain, or become, independent of the Tibetan (Dalai Lama's) Government" (1975b: 21).

I am a true son of Tibet beause I was born in Tibet in the state of Thingri. Moreover my parents were also true Tibetans. I have grown up til now under the guidance of His Holiness the Dalai Lama, who is the leader of Tibetans. So, I have grown up in the same manner as I have been fed. Moreover, I am practicing the Buddhist religion, which is the only religion of Tibetans. So, I am a true son of Tibet.

I think that I am a typical Tibetan boy even though I was born in India. Firstly, both my parents were Tibetan, and I have their blood. Secondly, I have the habits and customs that my forefathers have been practicing for hundreds of years. Besides that, my religion is also the same as theirs was. But there is a bit of change in my outer appearance, that is, in the way of dressing. It doesn't make any difference, as I think that my feelings, habits and customs are entirely different from those of an Indian boy.

I always introduce myself as a Tibetan because of the following reasons: (1) I was born in Tibet in 1958. (2) My parents and forefathers are also Tibetan. (3) I always do what my parents ask me to do. (4) I am under the spiritual leadership of His Holiness the Dalai Lama and I also worship him as a God. (5) I have adopted the religion of Buddhism which has enlightened Tibet and the Tibetan people from the very beginning of our civilisation. (6) I practice and preserve my religion, customs and traditions, and although I may look somewhat changed, it is because of the times and the situation.

In my opinion, to be a Tibetan means firstly one should be a Tibetan by birth, or his parents should be Tibetans. One should know what are his/her duties toward one's motherland. He should love his country. He should know the precious culture and traditions of his nation and should respect them. He should make some changes in the field of culture and tradition which suit the modern way of living. One of the most important things is that we should know our Tibetan language and literature. It is really shameful and unbecoming to a Tibetan if one doesn't know his language perfectly, being a citizen of Tibet. We should try to unite ourselves to make our nation

strong. Even if our country is not independent these days, we
should preserve our religion, culture and traditions and should
respect them at any cost. We should never forget that we are
Tibetans and we will get our country back from the clutches of
the Red Chinese, since Tibet belongs to Tibetans.

Several points in these responses deserve further comment: the intense nationalism; the fervent acknowledgment of the Dalai Lama
as a charismatic leader; the unique association of Buddhism with Tibetan identity; the focus on ancestral continuity; the emphasis on
language, traditions, customs, and what might be called "proper
modes of interaction"; and finally, the sense of cultural uniqueness.
The three admissions of cultural change, consciously justified in
two instances by reference to the times and the situation, are also
noteworthy in that they presuppose a qualitative difference between
essential and nonessential Tibetan attributes. Let me now analyze
these values and attitudes in more detail, focusing this time on the
implicit, rather than explicit, course of studies presented by these
schools: the cultivation of a Tibetan core and the maintenance of
interethnic boundaries.

Nationalism has only recently come to predominate over regionalism as a conscious sentiment and motive for loyalty among Tibetans. While some separatist inclinations still persist, particularly
among people from areas other than Central Tibet, the general feeling among people I talked with was that former intraethnic differences should not be allowed to divide a community in exile. In
addition, the "segmentary" pattern of uniting or defining oneself
against "the other" has shown all regional groups of Tibetans that
they do in fact share fundamental similarities, all the moreso in
comparison with China the aggressor and India the host country.

The schools, of course, are instrumental in promoting such attitudes. By means of the policies already considered—the ideological stress on pan-Tibetan unity in the textbooks, the discussions of
Tibetan religion and culture in regularly scheduled meetings, the
strongly traditional emphasis on the written language, and the fostering of cultural knowledge and pride through instruction and performances of Tibetan music and dance—students are taught to regard themselves as heirs of a distinct and noble tradition, which in

turn leads them to perceive their "feelings, habits, and customs" as being "entirely different" from those of Indians.

In addition to this lesson of proper demarcation between primary group and country of exile—an attitude encouraged in other ways as well—the schools also contribute to the development of a more militant type of nationalism simply by providing an official Tibetan context for what would otherwise be isolated statements coming from individual refugees. If, for example, a teacher expresses the belief that "we will get our country back from the clutches of the Red Chinese," the message in this case is not limited to the meaning of the sentence alone; students have no doubt already heard the same sentiments expressed privately, at home or among their peers. A teacher, however, is a respected authority figure hired by the Tibetan government; such a person speaks not ony as a private individual but as an officially endorsed educator. Political statements from such a source, then, tend to validate any similar ideas held privately, raising these to the level of officially sanctioned expressions of patriotism. When this is combined with actual deeds of patriotism such as the daily singing of the Tibetan national anthem, the staging of debates on the legitimacy of Tibet's claim to independence, and the schoolwide participation in the annual March 10 Uprising Day commemoration, the schools' role in the promotion of nationalism becomes even more evident. Positive sentiments of cultural uniqueness, national consciousness, and group loyalty are developed, fostered, and then channeled into an all-inclusive set of values and attitudes perceived collectively as "patriotism" (rgyal-zhen). This, in fact, is what motivates the desire to seek out and fulfill one's "duties toward one's motherland." By eleventh grade, students have already learned that a good part of their self-esteem as adults will come directly from their contribution to "the cause of Tibet."

Another significant feature of the student responses quoted, belief in the sacred charisma of the Dalai Lama as extraordinary leader, is particularly evident in the statement "I worship him as a God." While such an attitude, strictly speaking, does not coincide with orthodox Buddhist ideology, which recognizes neither God nor gods in an absolute sense, the sentiment of profound respect, if not actual worship, is nonetheless typical of the special regard Tibetans have for this unique figure. The image of the Dalai Lama that is deliberately and carefully presented in the schools is that of supremely precious leader of the Tibetan "race." As Yid-bzhin Nor-bu (a Tibetan title that may be loosely translated as "Wish-granting Jewel," suggesting omnipotent worth or preciousness), the Dalai Lama is respectfully incorporated into everyday school in much the same way as Chairman Mao figured in the socialization of Chinese children for three decades. His picture hangs in the center of the front blackboard in every classroom; his birthday is celebrated with much festivity by Tibetans all over the world; a prayer-song he wrote is chanted daily after the singing of the Tibetan and Indian national anthems; and prayers for his welfare are a constant aspect of regular worship services. Students in the upper grades read parts of his autobiography in Tibetan class, and everywhere one can see Dalai Lama buttons worn on jacket lapels. (These same jackets might additionally be sporting a hand-drawn picture of Bruce Lee on the back.)

So thorough is the indoctrination and so constant are the reminders of his status and beneficence (it was largely due to his international stature as a religious leader that worldwide attention was directed to the plight of Tibetan refugees immediately after 1959), that the phrase "by the grace of His Holiness" is very likely to precede any statement of progress achieved, health maintained, or benefits received. In fact, one of my last memories of my fieldwork site involves just this kind of "spontaneous" expression: the scene of a little boy playing alone on a windswept hilltop, shooting his slingshot and unselfconsciously singing a song about Yid-bzhin Nor-bu.

Another important aspect of ethnic self-definition can be seen in the fact that every single student who responded to my question mentioned religion, specifically Tibetan Buddhism, as an essential part of Tibetan identity. Not only do the comments all stress the continuity of religious tradition and practice, but in addition, one particular statement is especially significant: "Buddhism has enlightened Tibet and the Tibetan people from the very beginning of our civilisation."

The roots of this attitude can already be seen in early (ninth- and tenth-century) native texts that refer to "the little known country of barbarous Tibet," populated by "red-faced, flesh-eating demons," a self-description made "in relation to the civilizing influence of Buddhism" (Stein, 1972/1962: 40). A more critical view of this identification of "pre-Buddhist" with "precivilized" would also take into account the fact that the introduction and royal adoption of this religion coincided with "the first, but most important stage of the Tibetan Empire, the union or subjugation of the greater part of all the tribes or nations that by the Tibetans were considered as being of their own blood" (Haarh, 1969: 12).

The king at this time (r. 627–650), Srong-btsan sgam-po, is that very ruler who dispatched one of his ministers to India to bring back a writing system; like the much later succession of Dalai Lamas, he too is regarded by Tibetans as having been an incarnation of Tibet's patron bodhisattva, Avalokiteshvara. Srong-btsan sgam-po's patronage of a Tibetan alphabet—associated with the spread of Buddhism—can also be linked with the more secular developments of an emerging empire. According to an ancient Tibetan chronicle, the institution of writing was followed by the appearance of

> all the excellent texts of Tibetan custom, Tibetan sciences (or religions) and the great laws, the hierarchy of ministers, the respective powers of the great and the small (or of the elder and younger brothers), rewards for good deeds, punishments for evil and wrongdoing, and counting of skins for pasturelands and yokes for fields, equalization in the use of rivers, duties levied by (fixed) units of volume, weights, etc. (Bacot, Thomas, and Toussant, 1940–1946: 161, my translation)

Such an evident co-occurrence of newly established order and newly adopted religion lent itself perfectly to the scheme of the ecclesiastical historians who, as I have indicated, often wrote with the undisguised intention of promoting the greater glorification and spread of Buddhism. Given this orientation, which has become an established part of Tibetan historical consciousness, the introduction of Buddhism, viewed by Tibetans in retrospect, may be seen to correspond, in Lévi-Straussian terms, to the archtypical event that would have marked the passage from nature to culture, with cannibalism and chaos on one side, propriety and order on the other. Contemporary Tibetan evaluations of their own best qualities continue this association. As another student expressed it, "Tibetans are by nature a gentle, kind-hearted, gay and sympathetic people because of Buddhism."

As further explained by Tibetans, the basic virtue that underlies what is best about them is the predominant value of Buddhism, *snying-rje* [ɲiŋci,] "compassion." This word has an extensive range of usages in Tibetan. It is intimately associated with Avalokitesh-vara, the bodhisattva of mercy, and it figures prominently in Jataka stories (tales of the Buddha in his previous lives), which stress the supreme importance of taking pity on suffering beings. It is a part of Buddhist reverence for all forms of life, animal as well as human. In popular speech, the term *snying-rje* can also be applied to situations that rouse emotions of protective warmth or concern: seeing a piti-able beggar, sorrowful widow, lovable baby, or cuddly puppy, for example.

This kind of cultivated sensitivity—an openness to "being moved by compassion" (a stock scriptural phrase), an ability to identify, with sympathy and feeling, with all sentient creatures—lies at the heart of Tibetan values, and as such it figures prominently in the so-cialization of Tibetan children. The convergence of the two themes—collective identification with the Buddhist value of compassion and association of civil order with the taming of pre-Buddhist chaos—can be seen in the way Tibetan history is presented to Tibetan school-children. They are taught that it is the Buddhist religion that has made the qualitative, ennobling difference between light and dark-ness, order and chaos, those that have and those that have not been converted or tamed."[9]

The statement "Buddhism has enlightened Tibet and the Tibetan people from the very beginning of our civilisation" is thus express-ing an essential aspect of Tibetan self-evaluation, one in which "en-lightenment," with or without its metaphysical connotation, is re-garded as a criterion of being a fully realized human being. In the context of recent events, which have suddenly, even violently, forced a whole culture to confront new values and standards of excellence, this core belief in one's civilized, enlightened humanity has become even more meaningful: "Tibet has no oil deposits like Kuwait to boast about or machines like the West. Her sole pride and contribu-tion to the world is what she strove for and specialized in during the last 2000 years—*Tibetan Buddhism*" (Dawa Norbu, 1973: 9).

An additional, very evident feature of the students' self-definition as Tibetans relates to their focus on ancestral continuity: being born

9. The Tibetan word *'dul* means both to convert and to tame. It is the verb form of *'dul-ba*, "discipline, taming, conversion" (Das, 1970: 686), that translates the Sanskrit word *vinaya*, the title of the scriptures dealing with monastic discipline.

in Tibet, the land of their forefathers, or at the very least, being the offspring of Tibetan parents and "having their blood." This concern for native roots, parentage, and birth can certainly be seen by non-Tibetans, too, as one of the most basic criteria of ethnic belonging. In the Tibetan case, however, the factors of biological descent and genealogy represent only one possible aspect of a more complex and inclusive concept: *rgyud-pa* [küüpə], which can be translated loosely as "lineage."

Das's Tibetan-English dictionary (1970) glosses this substantive as "extraction; lineage, belonging to a family or race; family," and then goes on to explain *rgyud-pa gsum*: "the three kinds of lineage are (1) *gdung-rgyud*—family; descent; personal; (2) *sku-rgyud*—descent (as in the case of incarnate lamas); (3) *slob-rgyud*—spiritual descent (ministerial succession by disciples)" (p. 318). The verb *rgyud-pa*, which is glossed as "to tie, fasten, connect together," occurs in nominal form as *rgyud*, "a string, chain; that which joins things together; a connection, whether mental or physical" (p. 318); and all these words are related to another substantive, *brgyud*, which Das glosses as "(1) family, lineage, ancestors, offspring; (2) race, people, nation" (p. 342). In all these cases, then, "continuity" is essentially bound up with an actual entity, "mental or physical," that is connected or "enchained" in successive links. It is precisely this substantive aspect that serves to distinguish the three types of "lineages."

The first type, *gdung-rgyud* ("progeny, descendants"), refers to the continuity of the family line in accordance with the ordinary concept of genealogy. The word *gdung* by itself, an honorific term glossed as "(1) bones or remains of a deceased person; (2) family, descendants" (Das, 1970: 660–661), also suggests a patrilineal orientation inasmuch as the concepts "bone" (*rus* in nonhonorific Tibetan) and "flesh" (*sha*) serve to distinguish patrilineal relatives (*rus-rgyud*) from matrilateral affines.[10] Be that as it may, it is this first aspect of ancestral continuity, *gdung-rgyud*, that is most evident in the students' focus on Tibetan parentage as an essential criterion of their ethnic identity.

For these young people, many of them orphans, and some, the sole

10. With respect to all these kinship terms, it must be emphasized that no single, conclusive scheme has yet been worked out to account for the entire Tibetan system, which would include centuries of particular historical and regional usages.

survivors of what they regard as their family's "line," concern for "lineage" continuity is marked by a deep sense of urgency. This is further intensified by what they learn of their relatives and "race" (*brgyud*) left behind in Tibet. From the accounts of recently escaped refugees published in the Tibetan press, from corroborating accounts of Tibetans (some, new citizens of Western countries; others, still technically refugees residing in India or Nepal) returning from recently permitted trips to Tibet to visit relatives there, and at meetings held after school to keep all informed about "the situation in Tibet," students are constantly hearing of the imminent threat to their continued existence as a distinct ethnic group: "The Chinese are practicing genocide against our people in Tibet."

This charge has in fact been substantiated on several counts by an independent group of judges, professors, and practicing lawyers, the Legal Inquiry Committee on Tibet, who investigated statements and evidence from both Tibetan and Chinese sides "in a detached and juridical manner" and made known their findings in *Tibet and the Chinese People's Republic* (1960).[11] The report begins with the definition of genocide recognized by Article II of the United Nations Convention for the Prevention and Punishment of Genocide:

> In the present Convention, genocide means any of the following acts committed with intent to destroy, in whole or in part, a national, ethnical, racial or religious group as such: (a) Killing members of the group; (b) Causing serious bodily or mental harm to members of the group; (c) Deliberately inflicting on the group conditions calculated to bring about its physical destruction in whole or in part; (d) Imposing measures intended to prevent births within the group; (e) Forcibly transferring children of the group to another group. (p. 11)

The conclusion of this report, substantiated by over 300 pages of statements and appendices, does support many of the charges made by Tibetans. Four different types of evidence are cited, which, in the words of the committee, "reveal . . . an attempt to destroy the Tibetan part of the Buddhist religious group by two methods [(a) and (e) above] which fall specifically within the terms of Article II of the Convention for the Prevention and Punishment of Genocide" (p. 14).

11. For a critical interpretation of this report's objectivity as well as much of Sino-Tibetan historiography in general, see Grunfeld (1981).

As a result of this threat, Tibetans of all ages feel a deep responsibility to keep their culture alive, a goal that underlies the Tibetan government's encouragement of endogamy and a high birth rate. Actually, in India the first of these policies needs little official promotion, for both Tibetans and Indians generally perceive themselves as so very different from each other that marriage between the two groups hardly represents a real option. But the constantly reiterated slogan of the Indian government's birth-control program—"A small family is a happy family"—does, if only verbally, challenge the Tibetan government's desire for a high birth rate among its people. Yet the students in the Tibetan schools, though exposed to innumerable radio commercials, billboards, and posters, all extolling the benefits of limiting family size, nonetheless have their way of thinking already decided in the other direction before they graduate. As one eleventh grader put it, "Family planning may be beneficial for Indians because there are so many of them. But our people are being killed in Tibet, so we should be increasing, not limiting our population."

This personal concern for Tibetan continuity in the ordinary sense of genealogy (*gdung-rgyud*) represents only one of the three types of lineages mentioned earlier. The second type, which Das (1970) lists as "*sku-rgyud*—descent (as in the case of incarnate lamas)" (p. 318), refers to the Tibetan concept of *bla-rgyud*, the succession of lamas who continue to be reincarnated.[12] I have already indicated how this principle operates in the institution of the Dalai Lama, who is regarded as the direct reincarnation of his immediate predecessor and the indirect reincarnation of Avalokiteshvara, Tibet's patron bodhisattva. The same principle is also evident in the case of many high ecclesiastical figures, in particular, those associated with various Tibetan monasteries.

Exile in India has apparently not ended this type of continuity, although accounts in the Tibetan press indicate that the reincarnations tend to be "discovered" at a much later age than two or three, which was usual in Tibet. At my fieldwork site, the local ne'er-do-well, a character referred to by everyone as "really sdug-can" ("bad,

---

12. Actually, the term Das identifies as descent "in the case of incarnate lamas," *sku-rgyud*, is today used as an honorific for *rgyud*, that is, "lineage" in the sense of genealogy (*gdung-rgyud*). The term *bla-rgyud* is applied to the continuous succession of incarnations.

terrible, horrible"), used to drop in occasionally to bum cigarettes from me. In the course of one of his visits, he told me what I thought was a fantastic story: his younger brother had been recognized as a high incarnation by one of the Dalai Lama's tutors, who had had a clairvoyant vision that this particular boy would be found living "in a green house between two mountains in a family of two sons and two daughters." To my amazement, when I checked his story with my Tibetan friends, I found it to be true. By all accounts, the young man, 18 years old when I heard about him, had been "discovered" at age 14 and has since traded his former role, that of a teenage student at an elite Anglo-Indian school, for the role of a young incarnate lama committed to years of religious study, meditation, and pious living.

The third kind of "lineage" mentioned by Das (1970)—*slob-rgyud* (lineage of disciples)—refers to the well-established Indian and Tibetan tradition that emphasizes the very special relationship of continuity between teacher and disciple (*guru* and *chela* in Sanskrit; *bla-ma* and *slob-ma* in Tibetan). The important "substance" that is communicated and passed down in this case is oral teaching, particularly that which relates to mystical experience. Speaking of the "spiritual continuity linking teacher and disciple," Tibetologist Tucci (1970) notes further that "the two are joined together as links in a chain, guaranteeing an uninterrupted continuation of the teaching and the mystical experience" (p. 59, my translation).

Even while still in secondary school, not as yet critical of the phenomenon of Tibetan gurus traveling to teach at Western dharma centers, Tibetan students are keenly aware of the role their culture is playing in keeping alive this uninterupted continuation of the teachings of their religion. In this connection, a news item that appeared in the Indian press during the time of my fieldwork filled them with pride: a committee appointed by the Government of India was to begin work on a project to restore lost Sanskrit religious-philosophical texts by retranslating them from centuries-old, still-extant Tibetan translations. This modern-day acknowledgment of their culture's role in faithfully preserving religious-scholarly tradition is particularly meaningful to Tibetans living in India, who, having lost their connection with their homeland, have somewhat ironically become exiles in the land of their religion's founder. As in the cases of the continued recognition of reincarnated lamas and the uninterrupted attempts to maintain genealogical continuity, here too the concern for *rgyud* or *brgyud* emerges as an evident value within the total framework of Tibetan self-definition.

An additional set of attitudes and values Tibetans perceive as distinctly Tibetan involves what might be termed "proper modes of interaction," or "respectful behavior" (*ya-rabs spyod-bzang*), which can be associated in particular with certain sociolinguistic aspects of the Tibetan language. First, a language like Tibetan, spoken in a multiethnic society such as India, will almost automatically act as a distinct boundary marker, demarcating those of one's group from all others. Second, and this is where "respectful" or "proper" behavior is even more relevant, social demarcation is also made possible within the ethnic group by virtue of a particular feature of Lhasa-dialect Tibetan: the socially obligatory patterns of honorific speech, which can be manipulated to express proper respect or, secondarily, humorous debunking, deliberate obscuration, or deft sarcasm.

In terms of the boundary marking function, the issue is quite straightforward: children are taught by adults as well as peers not to mix Hindi and Tibetan in the same speech event. The relative strengths and weaknesses of this indoctrination can be observed in the minidramas that regularly occur when the purists among them lightly slap the wrists of their peer-group offenders. The offense is typically a word perceived as Hindi such as *baiskop* ("movies") or *retiyo* ("radio") inserted into a Tibetan sentence. The "problem" seen here by the purists—a too-ready acceptance of loan words—is countered by them with this attempted solution: periphrastic definitions used to create the new words now needed in Tibetan. Accordingly, "radio" is *rlung-'phrin* ("wind-news") and "movies" *glog-snyan* ("interesting electricity") in Tibetan.[13] Such attempts to stem the tide of foreign words will probably fail on an item-by-item basis, but the overall consciousness that is cultivated by such a policy ap-

---

13. Almost all these examples are in fact problematic with respect to their real etymology. *Baiskop* is actually a loanword into Hindi from the English "bioscope," and *retiyo*, too, derives originally from English. Although M. Goldstein's dictionary (1975a: 219) gives *glog-brnyan* as the "correct" spelling for the Tibetan word for "movies," it is significant that a Tibetan college student gave me not only *glog-snyan* (same pronunciation) but the folk-etymological explanation "interesting electricity." (The morpheme *snyan* means "interesting.")

pears to be working. The India-born generation is very much aware of the power of language, specifically their Tibetan language, to define their identity as a distinct ethnic group.

As for the honorific aspect of Lhasa-dialect Tibetan, the full range of its secondary symbolic possibilities (debunking, obscuration, or sarcasm) does not find much expression in the schools, at least not among the students. For them, the most important implications of *zhe-sa* (honorific speech) lie in its primary function: expressing various shadings of proper respect. For this reason, the deliberate teaching of the honorific language, both inside and outside the classroom, represents much more than linguistic pedagogy. For Tibetans, being respectful is a core value that characterizes fully human, thoughtfully humane behavior. What this ideally implies is a constant awareness of the other person vis-à-vis oneself, and it is precisely this kind of a dialectical interpersonal relationship that typifies the socially correct manipulation of honorific speech.

Briefly, the system works like this: "nouns, pronouns, verbs, and a few adjectives have two forms, honorific (h) and nonhonorific (nh). In third-person speech referring to two different individuals, there are thus four possible ways of expressing the statement, depending on the relative status of the persons involved. For example, the sentence, "He gave him a (Tibetan) dress" can be realized in any one of these ways:

khong-gis	*khong la*	*na-bza'*	*phul-gnang-pa red*
He (h)	to him (h)	dress (h)	gave (giver [h], recipient [h])
khong-gis	*kho la*	*na-bza'*	*gnang-pa red*
He (h)	to him (nh)	dress (h)	gave (giver [h], recipient [nh]
khos	*khong la*	*na-bza'*	*phul-pa red*
He (nh)	to him (h)	dress (h)	gave (giver [nh], recipient [h]
khos	*kho la*	*phyu-ba*	*sprad-pa red*
He (nh)	to him (nh)	dress (nh)	gave (giver [nh], recipient [nh])

In first- and second-person speech, however, the word choice signifying status is almost always predetermined by the "rule" of respect, which takes precedence over the objective status of the two persons involved. Accordingly, I the speaker should always refer to myself with nonhonorific nouns and verbs; the person I am address-ing is properly referred to in *zhe-sa*. This brief explanation greatly simplifies all the possibilities that could occur in an actual speech event; two good friends could, in fact, choose not to use *zhe-sa* at all, and there would be no disrespect involved. Nevertheless, the point remains: the socially correct use of *zhe-sa* implies an obligatory at-tention to social distance as well as dialectical appraisal of oneself in relation to the other. Whenever the honorific potential of the Ti-betan language is activated, then, the key Tibetan values of respect and propriety are further attended to, nourished, and reinforced.

Finally, all these characteristics—nationalism, special regard for the Dalai Lama, particular identification with Buddhism, concern for continuity, and emphasis on the Tibetan language—contribute together to the strong sense of cultural uniqueness so much a part of Tibetan young people's ethnic self-definition. To them, the influ-ence and borrowings from Tibet's two great neighbors, China and In-dia, appear either "superficial," (as in the examples of Chinese cui-sine and brocade and other penchants of the Tibetan aristocracy, or "significant," but adapted "according to the native genius" of Ti-betan culture, as in the case of Indian Buddhism (Dawa Norbu, 1973: 8). The schools' role in promoting such attitudes involves more than the explicit means and media of education. Besides directly convey-ing specific cultural information through officially organized in-stitutions and activities, this environment also serves to transmit a whole set of definitely focused, though less consciously communi-cated, values and attitudes. In terms of the expressed goal of foster-ing a strongly Tibetan Buddhist identity among the students, this implicit curriculum of the Tibetan school system is no less impor-tant than the explicit one.

Goals and Implications of Education in a Tibetan Environment

From the very first year of their people's exile in In-dia, Tibetan policy makers have given top priority to the formal schooling of the younger generation, hoping in this way to achieve several interrelated goals. Foremost among these is the broadly con-ceived aim of insuring the continued viability of Tibetan culture.

Not only do policies designed to implement this objective serve to promote various aspects of traditional Tibetan ideology; they also have the latent consequence of causing key ideological concepts to expand and thereby accommodate new problematic situations.

This last assertion warrants consideration at another level of discourse too: manifest and latent meanings are very much a part of the whole enterprise of anthropologizing. In summarizing this chapter, then, it is appropriate for me to direct some attention to the broader hermeneutic issues surrounding the ethnographic case at hand. The final part of these concluding remarks thus goes beyond a recapitulation of the Tibetan material regarding the transmission of essentially traditional, potentially open key symbols. Once more, I attempt to speculate more reflectively about the process of seeing, noting, and presenting such "data," this time in reference to this question: What is it in my own academic, historical, and personal tradition that prompted me to be more or less satisfied with the observations and interpretations I "made" and have presented here?

Before proceeding to these last considerations, however, a final review of this chapter's ethnographic focus is in order. In this connection, the comments of a junior official of the Council for Tibetan Education may serve as an appropriate point of departure. In response to my questions about the specific purposes of this organization's policies, this young man named three different objectives and then described each in relation to two touchstones: Tibetan Buddhist beliefs and the current exigencies of life in India today.

According to him, the first aim of education should be "to lead people to happiness, which is the desire of every sentient being." This preeminently Buddhist statement, which in fact echoes the words of the Dalai Lama on this subject, he further clarified by referring to the core values of compassion (snying-rje) and "emptiness" or selflessness, that is, the cultivated attempt "to eradicate selfishness; to act for the benefit of all creatures." Strictly speaking, of course, Buddhist theory does not talk of "happiness," but rather of the negation of its opposite, the elimination of suffering. As explained by this young man, education can accordingly contribute to this end by providing "the right view," that is, by offering a counterperspective that would replace craving with contentment, attachment with renunciation.

But in addition to this ideological explanation, evidently based on the Buddhist doctrine of the Four Noble Truths and the Eightfold Path, this person also spoke of "happiness" in more mundane terms, in relation to the grim economic realities of the employment situation in India. "Modern youth thinks that education will automatically bring a good job. When this doesn't happen, they become disappointed. Unlike Tibetans of the older generation who may have been poorly educated but who were content with their lives, many young people today are dissatisfied and unhappy."

While this young official did try to suggest a solution to the problem in terms of ideology ("We must integrate our traditional Buddhist values with modern education"), it is also clear that the Council for Tibetan Education is attempting to deal with the situation on a practical basis as well. I have described how the schools were initially established, with immediate attention given to the implementation of a modern curriculum, followed by a concerned search for qualified teachers. The mandatory cocurricular activity of work experience as well as the vocational orientation fostered by the 10 + 2 system also focuses squarely on the economic problems students are likely to encounter after high school. In this respect, then, the expressed goal of promoting "happiness" is not only ideological in nature but closely associated with the eminently practical concern for livelihood.

A second goal of the Tibetan education system is that of "eliminating superstition, or *rnam-rtog.*" This Tibetan term, which can also be glossed as "unreal conclusions" or "doubt" (Das, 1970: 759), has a special meaning in Buddhist philosophy: "discursive knowledge" based on the (false) dichotomization between a thinking subject and a thought-about object (Tucci, 1970: 81, 106, my translation). As explained by the young official, however, the elimination of "superstition," or *rnam-rtog,* is directly related to the cultivation of an educated critical-mindedness that would ideally replace "blind faith" with a properly reasoned religious affirmation.

But once again, the ideological concept—*rnam rtog* in this case—can also be interpreted so as to relate directly to a very real and current problem facing Tibetan youth. The deliberate introduction of scientific subjects into the curriculum represents a significant attempt on the part of the Council for Tibetan Education to familiarize students with rationalism, which is perceived as the prevailing intellectual philosophy of the modern world. Needless to say, the transition between old and new ways of thought can be difficult, involving what one young Tibetan has described as "inner personal conflicts, especially between the traditional norms and the scientific spirit" (*Tibetan Review*, 1973c: 3). But in an orthodox philosophical sense, Buddhism has never been antirational, and in this connection it is significant that the young official I talked with put so much stress on the "reason-affirming" aspects of the Tibetan language textbooks, which introduce upper-grade students to the traditional intellectual exercises of dialectic logic (*rig-lam*). The promulgation of such sophisticated philosophical techniques at the high school level is thus likely to continue, despite the occasional protests in the Tibetan press by students who claim that such texts are "overly emphasized" or "difficult to understand" (*Tibetan Review*, 1973a: 9, 10). In fact, such a means of trying to eliminate *rnam-rtog* actually serves two purposes; in addition to its ideal function of promoting critical thinking, the teaching of dialectical logic in high school also serves to remind young Tibetans that their intellectual tradition, too, has historically put great emphasis on sophisticated, highly elaborated reasoning techniques.

A third goal of this educational system is the constantly reiterated aim of preserving and promoting Tibetan culture and tradition. This goal was likewise clarified for me in reference to the ideal of compassion or service to others: "Our tradition, which has kept intact the essential teachings of Lord Buddha, can be of benefit not only to Tibetans, but to the whole world as well." But here, the case is somewhat different. Instead of expanding some traditional ideological concept to accommodate a new situation, this third goal directly associates traditional values with their potential for worldwide beneficial assistance. Such international, or pan-national, consciousness has been a part of the Tibetan educational system ever since it was first established in India, a foreign country. Initial contacts with non-Tibetan teachers, administrators, short-term volunteers, and far-flung relief agencies have made all levels of Tibetan society aware of the world at large, not only as a potential source of friends, benefactors, and allies, but as an instructive arena where the dramas of other stateless peoples are played out for all who are able to catch the implications. In addition, many children in the Tibetan schools regularly correspond with foreign "sponsors" who, by contributing toward their education and writing them personal letters, are also giving their "godchildren" their own private window on life in a non-Asian context.

All of these situations help foster a global consciousness that contrasts sharply with the geographical and attitudinal insularity that characterized Tibet of old. For this reason, it is doubly significant that the goal of preserving and promoting Tibetan culture should be directly associated with its perceived ability to benefit the whole world. Although such an awareness of "others," transcending both ethnic and national boundaries, may still be quite in keeping with the traditional "compassionate" ideology, it is nonetheless hard to overlook the new political element here: as stateless refugees, the Tibetans in India and elsewhere in the diaspora really are world citizens now. Furthermore, this outward-looking attitude also involves an extremely important subjective corollary. When children are taught that their culture has such a unique potential for worldwide beneficial influence, they are also being given the most powerful reason of all to remain Tibetan: self-esteem, meaningful identity, and even a sense of mission are all intrinsic to the self-definition so carefully fostered by the supportive Tibetan environment of these schools.

In sum, then, all three of these general educational goals (leading people to "happiness," eliminating "superstition," and preserving Tibetan culture by sharing its attributes on a worldwide scale) are expandable in character. Like the two key symbols they buttress and from which they in turn derive support, these goals resist being confined to any one interpretation. Such openness to multivocality I have in fact, already pointed out, particularly in connection with the more traditional symbol presented to the students in these schools: the centuries-old institution of the transcendent-yet-immanent Dalai Lama. As for the more contemporary of the two key symbols, the motif of independence, at this stage of their social learning, Tibetan children and adolescents have yet to idealize *rangzen* outside of the context of the nonambiguous political goal of getting their country back. Their future life experiences, however, are about to modify this, and their formal education thus far has already set the stage for this amplification.

In not too different a manner, my own formal education (as well as my traditional and personal past) likewise predisposed me to be, in the research situation, more or less aware of, or blind to, various indications that this or that event, word, or action, was "significant." In my case, however, the interpretations had to be personally derived rather than group created and shared, for these interpretations were to be the basis for the independently researched dissertation I was to write and not the components of an ideal to be sought collectively. Yet I was also definitely aware of a communal aspect to the research process, too. Membership in this "community" came about, not by ethnicity, religion, or nationality, but by disciplinary training and intellectual tradition. I knew, for example, that I could (and even should) begin writing this chapter by presenting a summary of how the Tibetan schools were established and that in this section I could avail myself of the written sources on this subject.

I also knew, however, that a dissertation in anthropology could never be spun exclusively from such threads and fibers. In observing and writing, I was thus impelled to see and note that which "only" I as an anthropologist could see and note. At the same time, I had to bring these documented trophies back home in a form that my professional judges, beginning with my dissertation committee, could understand as anthropological.

In any case, my task was to capture the material and give it tangible shape through my own words. Given the nature of what was most often before my eyes at my primary research site (children, books, and teachers much more than richly elaborated rituals), I obviously set to work here, taking notes and thinking about these subjects before any others. Yet my own role as observer raises questions: If I had not had some previous familiarity with (and much interest in) ways of graphically representing and commenting about symbolic forms such as language and music, would the "significant" observations I have noted in this chapter have appeared so significant? What *is*, in fact, the ontological status of a chanted spelling rule or a four-way permutation of honorific–nonhonorific sociolinguistic patterns? Could whole account be a virtual, rather than a real, image, a reflection more of the observer than the observed? The hall of mirrors is evident again: such speculations on the nature of reality and illusion are, of course, central to Buddhist philosophy.

Chapter Three

The Interplay of Ideology and Experience

As I have shown, formal education in the Tibetan school system is characterized by a deliberate emphasis on the continued transmission of cultural symbols and values kept as traditional as possible, with a good deal of the learning still very closely tied to primary socialization. After graduating, however, high school students leave this extremely supportive ethnic milieu and begin to gain practical experience in the more pluralistic context of modern India. The ideals so carefully presented and nurtured in the Tibetan schools—"compassion" (*snying-rje*); "respectful behavior" (*ya-rabs spyod-bzang*); and group consciousness and solidarity, or "patriotism" (*rgyal-zhen*)—now begin to appear less given by virtue of Tibetan ethnicity and much more a matter of individual choice.

The key symbol summarizing all these values—the Dalai Lama—is still crucial to these young people's self-definition as "Tibetan"; likewise, these three ideals are in no real danger of being questioned or replaced in the foreseeable future. Nonetheless, the continued transmission of traditional ideology in toto becomes much more problematic for these school leavers, who must now inhabit a new, less understandable, and less ideal social world. In this context, and for these Tibetans in particular, the *rangzen* motif gains tremendously in significance, not at the expense of the Dalai Lama symbol, but rather in ways more directly related to three types of new challenges these youths must face: economic responsibility for their own and their immediate families' livelihood; more sustained intellectual encounters with nontraditional modes of thought; and political involvement in Tibetan as well as international realpolitik.

In a similar way, the antropologist must try to appropriate meaningful interpretations, to overcome the cultural estrangement that inevitably results when an alien is suddenly immersed in a new social world. Unlike the Tibetans, of course, anthropologists cannot be reified as a group that shares ethnicity, religion, hopes, and memories, so no single metaphorical image parallel to the *rangzen* motif is likely to emerge and develop in the fieldwork situation. Nevertheless, there were significant similiarities between my attempts as an anthropologist to understand, and Tibetans' attempts to do likewise. Both were dealing with bits and pieces of the strange and the familiar; both had to acknowledge or begin to recognize that we had in some way lost "the naiveté of the first certainty." In brief, both were struggling to forge viable links between previously unquestioned ideology and present social experience.

My primary focus in this chapter, too, is the Tibetans' situation and not that of the anthropologist. I am most concerned with the three types of challenges, economic, intellectual, and political, that Tibetan youths must face after leaving high school. In this connection I examine these problems: obtaining financial assistance (scholarships) for higher education; balancing the implications of group-centered ideology ("patriotism," "working for the people") against the demands of supporting one's immediate family; maintaining a viable degree of cognitive consistency; and confronting the realities of in-group and international realpolitik. I then relate the hermeneutic issues to this ethnographic material.

Suffice it to say at this point that my observations and interpretations regarding Tibetan post–high school experience were more often than not made in more emotionally engaging settings than classrooms, school grounds, and houseparents' homes. It was exciting to travel about north India for interviews and meetings; to fly south to see one of the agricultural settlements; to witness, talk with, and manage to photograph Tibetan hunger strikers quietly protesting outside the United Nations Information Centre in New Delhi; to eat and drink and talk passionately with people willing to share some of their hopes and beliefs and reservations with me. The philosophical question raised by all of this is once again more related to "guessing" than "validation": to what degree could my ontological world (and not just my social sympathies) be enlarged by such powerfully affecting encounters with the discourse of these others?

Post–High School Options and Activities

The options open to young Tibetans at the completion of their secondary school program are limited by several constraints, almost all of them economic. As a refugee population living in a developing country with economic woes of its own, the Tibetan community as a whole can hardly afford to offer higher educational opportunities to all its young members without qualification. Furthermore, few of the approximately 25 percent of the high school graduates who do continue their formal education are able to choose a profession solely on the basis of their individual interests and aptitudes.[1] Even if a student has proven his or her academic ability by achieving a qualifying score on the All-India Higher Secondary Examination, other factors play an essential role in determining the actual possibility and course of further studies: financial support, coming from funds channeled by the Tibetan government or a foreign relief agency or private sponsor; a felt need on the part of the Tibetan community (specifically, the government-in-exile) for more college-trained specialists in a particular profession; and finally, an opening or "seat" occurring at the proper college at a time when the student's own schedule of responsibilities permits him or her to take advantage of it. As one young man put it, "Having a definite goal guarantees nothing. So many other conditions must also fall into place, all simultaneously. Without this happening, you cannot realize your aim." This person, who scored third in his class at the University of Delhi and wanted to continue his B.A. major to become an agricultural economist, began teaching in a small Tibetan elementary school in an isolated settlement in eastern India shortly after I returned to the United States.

His situation, by no means unique, well illustrates the tangle of contingencies facing this first generation of college students and would-be students. While economic conditions among the Tibetan community have decidedly improved in the two decades of exile, government-allocated financial resources—in this case, the scholarships channeled through the Tibetan administration—are still a

---

1. This figure includes college and university students as well as trainees at modern vocational institutes and traditional Tibetan-run institutions such as the Tibetan Institute of Performing Arts and the Tibetan Medical Centre. For a more detailed presentation of the statistics on high school graduates, see Nowak (1978b: 228).

very scarce commodity. Accordingly, the issue of financial sponsorship for higher studies has engendered attitudes of tense resentment and suspicion in many young Tibetans. Coming from backgrounds of poverty, envisioning the barely subsistence wages that await most of them even if they do complete college, they are not unfamiliar with economic hardship. Moreover, they are quite ready to assume adult financial responsibility "for the cause of Tibet," or more personally, for the sake of an old, sick parent or younger, dependent cousin or siblings. What these young people fear, with respect to the allocation of scholarships, is thus not some new deprivation but a repetition of old patterns whereby the "haves" of yore might still get more than their due.

Some wealthy Tibetan families are in fact the object of particular resentment on this point. According to more than one source, several of them, having left Tibet early, with gold, then had their sons and daughters apply for—and receive—financial assistance for higher studies on the grounds that they were, after all, "poor refugees." For this reason, young Tibetans today regard their government's policies of appointments and allocations with wary concern, always on the lookout for any evidence of favoritism in general and nepotism in particular.

Correspondingly, the Tibetan administration has, since those first chaotic years of exile, attempted to announce and award scholarships according to a clearly publicized and equitable strategy. In a lengthy explanation—actually, a rejoinder to earlier criticism—the deputy secretary of the Council for Tibetan Education, Dawa Dhondup, (1976: 33) has stated that "the sole criterion for awarding scholarships is the order of merit in the schools' final result." This in fact corroborates what I was told by the rector of the residential school where I did my research: "The schools' final result" (referring here to the Higher Secondary Exam) serves to rank candidates into four ordered categories: first division, second division, "pass with compartments" (overall pass with failure in an individual subject), and failure. Students who obtain a first division pass (10 Tibetan students out of the 194 eleventh graders who took the exam did so in 1977; 25 out of the 181, in 1976) are then eligible to be chosen by the council to receive the 15 scholarships awarded annually by the government of India through the Central Tibetan Schools Administration.

In addition, other volunteer agencies, and some foreign individuals as well, also offer full or partial financial sponsorship for higher education. The German Academic Exchange awards about 10 scholarships, each worth 400 rupees per month, to Tibetan students who pursue higher studies in science. (The average monthly salary for young employees of the Tibetan government is only about 200–250 rupees, about U.S. $26 at the time I was in India). American and Swedish organizations also offer a small number of scholarships each year, and the Charitable Trust Office of His Holiness the Dalai Lama provides funds for promising but needy students. Finally, Swiss Aid to Tibetans represents the largest single source of financial assistance for the higher education of young Tibetans.

This latter agency is significant in another way, too. Although it does additionally sponsor the 6-month Tibetan Language Teachers Training Program through the auspices of the Council for Tibetan Education, its primary way of allocating support for higher studies is to deal directly with the students who request assistance. Decisions regarding these scholarships are thus not made by the council but by the Swiss director of Swiss Aid to Tibetans, who travels often to India and appears to be personally familiar with the individual backgrounds and abilities of many young Tibetans. I once witnessed an exchange between this man and a friend of mine who was about to complete her B.A. and hoped to do an additional year's study to earn a B.S. in education, a degree that in India takes 1 year longer to achieve than the B.A. She had hardly expressed her wish before the director began contemplating aloud: her scholastic record was excellent; her contribution as a teacher would be increased by this opportunity; the requisite program was offered by two different colleges, each with a different deadline date for admission. . . . Laconically but quickly he announced his decision: "I support you," he said. "Apply for admission as soon as you get your B.A. results."

The implications of this direct avenue of appeal, with its built-in ability to circumvent bureaucracy, are not lost on the young. I know of one case where a high school girl, desiring to transfer from the Tibetan school to a more elite Anglo-Indian institution, wrote a letter, intended to be secret, to her foreign sponsor, entreating the latter to help her attain her goal. In this particular case, other complications caused the plot to misfire, but the very fact that such an attempt was made shows that this girl was learning, however imperfectly, the intricacies of "proper" but efficacious appeal. In fact, the whole process of personally requesting financial aid for education, whether through the council or from an independent source, has the effect of teaching a primary lesson in adaptive strategy: individual initiative counts, especially in an economy of scarcity.

My discussion so far has considered those constraints and contingencies, mostly economic, that affect and limit the opportunities of the young Tibetans who would like to continue their formal education at various institutions of higher learning. While such a program of post–high school studies definitely represents, in their eyes at least, the preferred, prestigious ideal, it is by no means the only option that can provide further learning experience. Besides the standard academic programs offered by Indian colleges and universities, there are the modern vocational training course conducted at Pachmarhi (described in the previous chapter) and the various training programs for teachers, nurses, secretaries, and accountants; a special course for Tibetan language teachers is offered by the Central Institute of Higher Tibetan Studies. In addition, other Tibetan-run institutions provide instruction in traditional modes of Tibetan knowledge. Four of these—the Central Institute just mentioned, located in Sarnath; the Buddhist School of Dialectics, in Dharamsala; the Sakya College, in Rajpur; and the School of Buddhist Philosophy, in Leh, Ladakh—specialize in religious-philosophical programs of study. A fifth, the Tibetan Medical Centre, in Dharamsala, continues the tradition of the famous Chakpori (*lcags-po ri*) and Menze Khang (*sman-rtse khang*) medical and astrological colleges of Lhasa. A sixth, the Tibetan Institute of Performing Arts (formerly the Tibetan Music, Dance and Drama Society, or *bod-kyi zlo-gar tshogs-pa*), also of Dharamsala, instructs future teachers and performers in the music, dance, and folk operas of Tibet.

The Central Institute of Higher Tibetan Studies, inaugurated in 1967, was initially established as a center of learning where monk students would be able to study traditional Tibetan Buddhist philosophy in an atmosphere conducive to the practice of monastic routine. At the same time, certain departures from the old system of monastic education were also built into the program. Examinations were reorganized in accordance with the policies operative in modern universities, and scholars who completed their education there were assigned new jobs elsewhere, instead of staying on as was customary in Tibet (*Tibetans in Exile*, 1969: 198). In the beginning, the school was affiliated with nearby Varanasi (Benares) Sanskrit University, but this arrangement was intended to be a temporary one, lasting only "until such time as the Tibetans would be able to run the institute on their own" (*Tibetans in Exile*, 1969: 201).

That time has now arrived. A news item in the November 1977 issue of *Tibetan Review* (1977f: 10) noted that the administration of this institution was then about to be transferred to the governing body of the Central Tibetan Schools Administration. Two other changes are even more significant in terms of learning opportunities: the institute is now open to both male and female lay students as well as monks; and the study of traditional subjects is now being augmented, owing to the wishes of some deeply interested students, by serious investigation of Marxist social and economic theories.

The principal of this institute, a young but erudite monk scholar who is well versed in modern political ideologies as well as Buddhist philosophical studies, explained to me how this school tries to integrate both modern and ancient types of instruction. Students study English and Hindi as well as traditional subjects such as Sanskrit, Tibetan grammar, history, literature, and philosophy. In classrooms without Western chairs and desks, they sit cross-legged on the floor, and their teachers sit likewise on small rugs. The "classes," or levels of study, are referred to by Sanskrit terms associated with Indian Buddhism, titles that can be roughly correlated with the grades or degree programs of a modern educational system: *Madhyma*, corresponding approximately to the last 4 years of secondary school; *Shastri*, approximating the B.A. level; the *Acharya*, the M.A. level.

Such examples, of course, hardly prove of and by themselves that a viable integration of old and new, familiar and alien has been achieved. The institute is in fact, not without its problems in this respect. The five pioneer girl students who were enrolled there at the time of my visit told me how discouraged they felt about the difficulty of their courses. Their reaction, according to the principal, was typical of beginners in the program; but unlike the others in their class, these girls did not feel free to commiserate beyond their own small circle. They had no way, therefore, of knowing that they were not alone in their sentiments. Despite the principal's strong conviction that Tibetan women, too, should study and contribute to the field of Buddhist philosophy, these first female *Madhyma* students were more affected by the comments of older, conservative Tibetans living in the area: "If we talk to boys (especially to monks!), they tell us we're bad girls.'" When I returned to the United States, I received a letter from one of these students, telling me that all five of them have since left the institute to return to regular Tibetan secondary schools.

Given the radical change implied by these girls' very presence at such an institution, the outcome of this first attempt at integrating women in a Tibetan Buddhist philosophy program is probably not too surprising. Another problem faced by this school also has its roots in old, slow-to-die attitudes: the alleged predominance of Ge-lugpa students and teachers as compared with those of the other Buddhist sects.[2] Despite such difficulties, however, the Central Institute of Higher Tibetan Studies is nonetheless making an unprecedented contribution to the learning opportunities of young Tibetans, offering them a program of scholastic depth in an atmosphere of intellectual ferment and ongoing syncretism.

In contrast to the open-admissions policy of the institute at Sarnath, the Buddhist School of Dialectics at Dharamsala remains a strictly monastic institution that accepts as students only male novices from the various Buddhist sects. Established in 1972 to preserve the special religious-philosophical traditions (*mtshan-nyid*) of the Gelugpa sect, this school is particularly characterized by its emphasis on *rig-lam*, a sophisticated form of logical argumentation used for centuries to illustrate the Mahayana Buddhist doctrine of the Middle Path. In brief, this school of Mahayana Buddhist philosophy teaches that the phenomenal world is "real" only in a relative, qualified sense; what truly exists in an absolute, nonconditioned sense is Emptiness (*stong-pa nyid*). The ontological nihilism of this position can itself be challenged by its own logic, and this whole process of systematic argumentation (traditionally practiced in formalized "debates" between two monks) can be used, according to the principal of this school, "to penetrate those teachings of Lord Buddha which are most deep and most difficult to understand by ordinary study alone."

The 7-year program of studies, which begins for most young men after the completion of regular secondary school, concentrates on

2. See *Tibetan Review* (1976d, 1976f) for a full discussion of this criticism.

Buddhist logic, metaphysics, and philosophy; but apart from this, students are also encouraged to pursue standard B.A. and M.A. programs through correspondence courses offered by various Indian universities. This supplementary emphasis on modern subjects reflects the Council for Tibetan Education's desire that the emerging generation of young monks be capable of interacting with and teaching people who do not speak Tibetan. In view of current statistics and interests,[3] such concern does not seem at all misplaced. In fact, the School of Dialectics, located in what must be the world's capital for Westerners studying Tibetan Buddhism, thus offers its students both a formal program of studies and a raison d'être that is daily confirmed by the constant sight of Dharamsala's international dharma seekers. The principal himself implicitly recognized this when he explained the projected goals of this institute to me, enlisting the aid of a monk student interpreter, whose very presence further illustrated the point: "We hope to produce learned men who are familiar with both English and dharma. We are not teaching Buddhism as missionaries, but because it is very beneficial for all living beings; for peace and happiness. That is why we are studying dialectics: to give these teachings to the West."

Another Dharamsala institution, the Tibetan Astro-Medical Centre, is also consciously motivated by an ideal of service to the Tibetan community in particular and the world at large as well. Established separately in 1961, the Tibetan Medical Centre and the Tibetan Astrological Centre were incorporated in 1967, reflecting the close relationship that is held to exists between these two categories of traditional knowledge (e.g., specific rhythms of seasonal or monthly time are believed to have an effect on the efficacy of gathering and preparing medicinal herbs). In its present merged form, the centre aims to preserve and deepen the traditions of Tibetan medicine through research, which includes the further study of Tibetan medical and astrological texts and the comparative study of Western medical theories, particularly those concerning incurable diseases such as cancer. The chief physician at the time of my fieldwork, a

3. *Tibetan Review* (1976i) notes that "there are already 119 monasteries in exile, including 9 in the West." In addition, *Tibetan Review* (1979) lists 75 Tibetan Buddhist meditation and study centers outside India and Nepal: 47 in the United States; 3 in Canada, 4 in New Zealand and Australia; 8 in Great Britain; 6 in France; and 1 each in Sweden, Denmark, Switzerland, West Germany, Holland, Spain, and Italy.

woman who has lectured, via interpreter, on Tibetan medicine at several American universities, would diagnose and treat an average of 60–150 patients per day, Indians and foreigners as well as Tibetans. In addition to the dispensary where these activities are carried out, the centre also includes a medical college, a small hospital, and a pharmacy, where Ayurvedic medicines are prepared from the extracts of herbs, metallic compounds, and precious stones.

As of November 1977, the college had 15 students, including 4 young women. Their 7-year program of study follows the traditional Tibetan syllabus for this profession: medicine, astrology, grammar, poetry, and religion. In addition, students go on field trips to learn how to identify and collect the medicinal plants, and their last years of study are particularly devoted to a supervised internship, where they learn how to diagnose illness. The inclusion of grammar, poetry, and religion in the prescribed course of study reflects the fundamental difference between Western and Tibetan medical theory. According to Doctor Yeshi Dhonden (1976), the Dalai Lama's personal physician and former head of the Tibetan Medical Centre:

> Tibetan medicine, firmly rooted in religion and philosophy, takes man as a whole, in the empirical and transcendental aspects, as a physical entity and metaphysical potentiality. . . . While the cultivation of the art and science of medicine is predominantly intended to cure the physical ailments of a being, Tibetan physicians place an equal degree of stress on the cultivation and development of mental power and the observance of moral laws. (pp. 6–7, 5)

The effect of such a radically holistic perspective on humanity can result in diagnoses that are just as surprising, at least to an empirical particularist, as is the Tibetan physician's emphasis on "transcendental aspects" and "metaphysical potentiality." A good friend of mine, a Tibetan graduate student in physics, went to this dispensary for a check-up after numerous visits to a modern university hospital had failed to cure him of a persistent sinus aggravation. The Tibetan doctor, however, did not confine her investigations to the "obvious" source of the problem; in fact, she concluded that the real source of his illness was "in the bones" and would manifest itself later in his life as rheumatoid arthritis.

While this diagnosis may not have been particularly cheering or even immediately verifiable for my friend, he, like others with his educational background, was particularly interested in the broader theoretical basis of this approach. It allows for and even emphasizes multidimensional systematic associations that would not likely be considered in a medical examination based on observable and recounted symptoms alone. For many young, Western-educated Tibetans, in fact, it is precisely this aspect of traditional Tibetan medicine—its more inclusive sphere of relevant concerns—that prompts them to take a second look at this centuries-old institution. For some of them—curious or hopeful patients as well as uninvolved but interested observers—the Tibetan Astro-Medical Centre primarily offers an alternative or supplement to Western medical practice. For others, specifically the full-time medical students, the centre is likewise a full-time supporter and product of a systematized and comprehensive ideology of integration, culminating in the belief that "health is the proper relationship between the microcosm which is man and the macrocosm which is the Universe" (Yeshi Dhonden, 1976: 7). In terms of formal, post–high school learning opportunities, then, the medical college associated with this centre thus represents one of the most tradition-affirming options open to young Tibetans today.

The last organization in this general category of Tibetan-run institutes, the Tibetan Institute of Performing Arts (*bod kyi zlo-gar tshogs-pa*, often referred to simply as "Dhoegar" [*zlo-gar*], was officially established for two purposes. First, the traditions of singing and dancing, considered by Tibetans as a mark of "that inner contentment which is so characteristic of the Tibetan people," were regarded as "an indispensable part of Tibetan life" and therefore became an essential object of cultural preservation (*Tibetans in Exile*, 1969: 251). Second, Tibetans also saw the staged presentations of this tradition as a potential means of spreading positive propaganda: "We also needed to acquaint the world with our unique culture which had hitherto remained a mystery to them due to our having kept aloof from the rest of the world" (*Tibetans in Exile*, 1969: 251–252). The learning opportunities offered by this institute can be similarly classed according to these two orientations, relating either to the ideal concerns of the Tibetan community or to the more far-reaching implications of international realpolitik.

In the first case, the stated aim of the Dhoegar is by and large being achieved. Performers as well as future teachers for the Tibetan schools are being trained in the instrumental music, songs, dances, and folk operas of Tibet, thus guaranteeing that the next generation, at least, will have its own specialists to keep alive and continue these traditions. But this institution, which operates on a shoestring budget, is not without its problems. In an interview that appeared in another Tibetan publication, a bilingual (Tibetan and English) quarterly called *Rangzen*, which is put out by the Tibetan Youth Congress, a young actor, Phurbu Tsering (1976), has expressed his views on this subject:

> Even though the Government does provide for this Institution, they do not seem to realize the tremendous value and potential of the Dhoegar. The Administration uses the Dhoegar as a dumping ground for people that they have no other place to send. The Dhoegar never has enough money, and our staff and actors receive a very inadequate salary. Even a peon in a Government office receives a larger salary than one of our trained performers. . . . But the worst and most irritating problem is the incredibly stupid attitude that most Tibetans have toward actors and dancers. They think that it is a low profession. Due to all these difficulties many young people are discouraged from joining the Dhoegar. Even some of our own members have been forced to leave because of family pressure or financial difficulties. I do not feel I am stretching things when I say that it is a great tragedy for our nation when a talented actor, dancer or musician painstakingly trained for many years has to leave to find work in a factory all because of a few rupees. (pp. 22–23)

The opinion that "acting is a low profession" is one that is hardly unique to Tibetan society. Yet in the Tibetan case, the second stated aim for establishing the Dhoegar—"acquainting the world with our unique culture"—adds particular weight to the actor's criticism. The feeling of being insufficiently supported is intensified when official verbal praise only serves to highlight the gap between ideal goals and actual financial assistance.

More than any other organized group of Tibetans, the members of the Dhoegar have had the opportunity to present selected aspects of their culture to a worldwide audience. In addition to staging performances at their home location in Dharamsala, the Drama Society has also gone on tour, traveling in 1975/1976 through Europe, North America, Southeast Asia, and Australia under the sponsorship of a New York–based enterprise, Kozuko Hillyer International Inc. The 23 member troupe, most in their late teens or early to middle 20s, learned much from this experience, particularly with respect to the workings of international realpolitik. As described in *Tibetan Review* (1976a), two days before the group was scheduled to leave Switzerland for the United States,

> the American Embassy in Switzerland tried to take back the visas issued to the troupe, saying that there was "some mistake." The Tibet Office in New York had to approach the China desk in the State Department to [request them to] reconsider the decision of withdrawing the visas. This abrupt action of the State Department seems contradictory when it is remembered that earlier on the State Department, in response to vehement Chinese protests against the coming of the Tibetan drama troupe to the U.S.A., had replied that "the activities of the Tibetans were in accord with the constitution and laws of the United States." Clearly there was some outside pressure put on the State Department. (pp. 11–12)

In addition, the U.S.-China People's Friendship Association picketed and distributed pamphlets outside performances in Berkeley, Ann Arbor, Madison, Washington, D.C., and New York City (*Rangzen*, 1976b: 18). These leaflets elaborated the Chinese point of view: Tibet belongs to China, and those Tibetans who say otherwise are traitorous, upper-class reactionaries. Given the opportunity to respond to such criticism, the Tibetan manager and interpreter for the Dhoegar countered the charges in several TV and press interviews, "the honesty of which," according to him, "convinced far more people of the truth of our cause than the hollow lies of Peking" (*Rangzen*, 1976b: 18). Be that as it may, this entire group of young Tibetans was unquestionably affected by the tour, which can be most aptly described as multilevel political theater. In fact, by publicizing these experiences via the Tibetan press, the members of the Tibetan Institute of Performing Arts are doing more than just acquainting the

world with their unique culture; they are also contributing significantly to the entire Tibetan community's growing familiarity with
the public relations tactics of international politics.

In addition to the two general types of post–high school options
and activities I have already discussed (formal education at Indian
colleges, universities, and training centers, and enrollment in various Tibetan-run institutes), one other very broad category of instructive experience remains open to Tibetan youth: employment,
whether this be in a salaried position under the auspices of the Tibetan government-in-exile, private enterprise, or agricultural work
at one of the Tibetan settlements.

The first of these actually includes two possible types of jobs:
working directly for the Tibetan government in one of its offices or
teaching in one of the Tibetan schools. Neither of these situations
offers much financial remuneration, so this type of employment
tends to be initially regarded by idealistic high school students as
the way of supporting oneself and being patriotic at the same time.
Reality intrudes quickly, however, and the views of those who have
already begun such work, or who are just about to do so, are much
more critical. First, there are the predictable problems caused by
a new type of applicant: college educated, yet automatically subordinated to older, more traditionally experienced officials. As one
young man expressed it:

> as a Tibetan, I'm better off than most, but in our society
> there's nothing to look forward to except being a teacher in a
> Tibetan school or a clerk in a Dharamsala office. And if I do
> become a clerk, even with a master's degree, nobody will think
> any more of my opinion than if I had no degree at all.

Another young man, employed in a Tibetan government office in
Delhi, admitted to me that it is a real temptation for him not to
strike out on his own after having received specialized secretarial
training in Calcutta. In fact, he had even had a private interview
with the Dalai Lama about his plans; he would prefer to work in
Ladakh (a cold, bleak region in northern India), where he could put
his expertise and initiative into practice, rather than remain in Delhi
stuffing envelopes. For the time being, however, he was going to stay
at his present post, justifying this to himself in terms of patriotic

commitment ("I *do* believe in what I'm doing") and qualifying it by limiting the duration ("In another 2 years I'll see. . . .").

The issue of "working in Ladakh" in fact represents much more than a preference for this, rather than that, job location. This desolate region, restricted until 1975, was therefore unable to receive assistance from foreign relief agencies before that time. Approximately 4,000 Tibetans were living there when I was in India, most in extreme poverty; thus for some young, educated Tibetans, Ladakh has become the focus for idealistic slogans about "working to help our people." Others, however, see volunteer work in such conditions as being all too much like taking up "a second exile" (*Tibetan Review*, 1976: 4). One individual explained the different attitudes to me in this way:

> It is the more [economically] privileged Tibetans who are the first to proclaim such a cause, but in the end, they are likely to find some excuse not to do it. On the other hand, those of us who have "grown up in difficulty" know enough to shirk such activity if possible, but in the end, even though we wouldn't volunteer for it, we *would* do it.

While Ladakh might be the proving grounds of idealism par excellence, a much more common test of young teachers' and clerks' loyalty to the Tibetan community is simply their willingness to continue in the system, month after month, for the same low wages. This is particularly the case with young government workers, who, unlike the teachers hired and paid by the Central Tibetan Schools Administration, are not subsidized at all by the Indian government. This point is emphasized in an editorial appearing in the December 1976 issue of *Tibetan Review*. Its author, Tsering Wangyal, begins by describing the types of people that can be found in this situation:

> A member of this establishment falls in any one or various combinations of the following categories: Those who are sincerely desirous of helping the people; those who aspire to a position of rank and respectability, which does not necessarily come in the way of working sincerely; those who want to try it out and see if it is more interesting than all the other occupations they have tried; and those who just fulfill the requirements to fit in Dharamsala and not anywhere else. Financial

reward has never been an incentive in Dharamsala. Tibetan Government officials are perhaps less well off materially than any other people, including most other Tibetans. (Tsering Wangyal, 1976: 4)

For both groups of salaried employees—teachers and government workers—the idealistic aim of working for the people faces a stiff challenge from social and economic realities. For a young, educated person, a job at a large school in Mussoorie, Darjeeling, or Dharamsala also implies the possibility of living near friends of a similar age and educational background; Ladakh-motif to the contrary, it is these places that get far more applicants than small day schools in various remote settlements. For young clerical workers, poorly paid and usually at the bottom of the status ladder, the motivation is similar; they are much more likely to "scramble for government posts" (*Tibetan Review*, 1977b: 4) than to continue expending all their energy on that idealistic goal of working for the Tibetan community. In both of these cases, the situation of employment teaches hard lessons of practicality, realism, and compromise with untested idealism.

For those who make their living by engaging in private enterprise, circumstances are somewhat different: in most cases, the element of economic risk is greater, but so too are the perceived changes for a Horatio Alger success story. In fact, the present editor of *Tibetan Review* told me that it is private enterprise that represents the greatest source of personal income for Tibetans in India. This category includes everything from large-scale, high-risk ventures such as restaurant management, sweater selling, and major investment in Tibetan marketing schemes (e.g., selling and exporting Tibetan carpets) to part-time petty trading. In the first case, where the initial capital investment usually necessitates borrowing (most often from a kin-based network), the would-be entrepreneur must first pay back the loan before any profit can be realized.

The activity of sweater selling offers a good illustration of how this works. As explained to me by a young man who had himself engaged in this venture alone at age 17, first he had to borrow 6,000 rupees (approximately U.S. $780) to buy the Indian-made sweaters and shawls from the factory in Ludhiana (an industrial city in northern India). Then he set out with his wares, following the seasonal climate changes (going down to south India during their cool season, then returning to the hill stations when the rest of India became hot). At the end of the selling season, he paid off his creditors and kept the profit of several hundred rupees, which would support him and his old, sick mother until his next commercial venture.

Such a way of life, with its built-in mobility and its alternation of busy season with slack periods, appeals to few other ethnic groups in India, especially as non-Tibetans who own even a little piece of land are loath to leave it, even temporarily. For the landless Tibetans, however, sweater selling has become an occupation they have virtually monopolized, all over India. Furthermore, the life style that necessarily accompanies itinerant selling and trading does not involve any conflict with traditional sex roles; Tibetan women, at least traditionally, have been among the most independent in Asia. Wives have long been regarded as equal to, or more capable than, their husbands in their ability to manage and control money, and the temporary separations sometimes occasioned by this activity are not considered threatening by or to either sex.[4]

In comparison with more sedentary types of private enterprise (e.g., managing a restaurant or small shop; engaging in local trading), sweater selling from bazaar to bazaar all over India is definitely a more striking occupation, and indeed, the adaptive strategies used by these people could easily become the subject of a complete study in its own right. From my perspective, however, this activity is instructive insofar as it serves as a learning experience for the whole Tibetan community. Those who actually make their living by sweater selling or other forms of private enterprise of course learn a great deal about risk, profit, and loss in particular and about economically motivated human nature in general. But in addition, even those Tibetans who support themselves in some other way are still affected, in terms of collective self-image, by that segment of their own population that engages in private enterprise, on whatever level.

Tibetans readily describe themselves as "born horse traders" (*Tibetan Review*, 1973e), but their attitude toward this self-acknowl-

4. The traditional independence of Tibetan women appears to be giving way to a more dependent style of femininity, obviously influenced by, if not modeled after, sex role expectations in Indian society. For a more complete discussion of changing sex roles among young Tibetans in India, see Nowak (1980).

edged stereotype is ambiguous. On the one hand, they sincerely admire economic savoir faire, thus revealing some of that "extraordinary pragmatism" Snellgrove and Richardson, (1968: 236) noted in another context. While I was walking through a bazaar with some Tibetan college girls, I passed a group of sweater sellers who were carrying on an animated conversation in Hindi with prospective Indian customers. At this, one of the young women turned to me and said, with a touch of quiet pride, "You never see *our* people begging." On the other hand, Tibetans have also expressed the fear that "hustling" (a word used commonly by English-speaking Tibetans) can go too far. A young man put it this way: "When you're a full-time hustler, you become after a while so willing to trade anything that you trade a lot of other things too. At that rate, if people just stick to hustling, they can never get back a free country." Such attitudes toward aggressive private enterprise, both pro and con, are particularly significant for the young generation, which is trying to make peace with the oftentimes conflicting demands of single-minded youthful idealism and realistic respect for pragmatic adaptability.

Other types of employment have also provided Tibetan young people with opportunities to observe, learn, and thereby shape or modify their personal conception of their ethnic identity. In 1966 a small-scale industrial program, the Tibetan Industrial Rehabilitation Society (TIRS), was established to create jobs for nonskilled or semiskilled Tibetans in such projects as working on tea estates or at a limestone quarry, a lime-producing factory, a woollen mill, and a fiberglass plant (*Tibetans in Exile*, 1969: 95–102). By 1973 these attempts were so fraught with problems that headlines in the Tibetan press appeared to be announcing the program's imminent and total collapse: "TIRS: Not a Success Story" (*Tibetan Review*, 1973f), and "The Tearful Tales of TIRS" (*Tibetan Review*, 1973d). One result of this experimental program has, however, been succssful: TIRS has redirected its orientation from an industrial focus to one emphasizing settlements that are "agriculture-based, supported by handicrafts" (*Tibetan Review*, 1973d: 7).

These handicraft centers, where Tibetan workers are trained and paid on a piece rate or monthly basis, have been established in the various Tibetan settlements all over India. The products made there—carpets, jackets, Tibetan aprons, belts, boots, and other traditional items—are sold on location or in cities like Darjeeling or

Delhi, where foreign tourists are likely to visit. The workers, men and women of all ages, are usually people who have had limited or no formal education. The management positions, however, are most often filled by young adults who know English, and the whole enterprise can easily serve as a temporary toehold, so to speak, for ambitious but impecunious people on their way up from carpet-weaving apprentice to All-India Marketing Man of the Year, an award won by a Tibetan in 1977.

The communal aspects of these handicraft centers (workers are in many cases provided with housing, Tibetan schools, and day-care centers for their children) are even more characteristic of the last type of employment I consider here: the agricultural settlements themselves. A complete description of these planned, flourishing Tibetan communities would take me far afield from my focus on post–high school options and activities; in passing, however, there are a few important points to note.

The first of these settlements was established in 1960, one year after Tibetans had begun arriving in great numbers at the temporary transit camps established for them in Assam and West Bengal (northeastern India). As part of a large-scale rehabilitation program worked out by the Indian government and assisted by international relief agencies, thousands of acres of unused land were leased by the state governments to Tibetan settlers through the administrative network of the Dalai Lama's unrecognized but de facto government. These settlements, which are concentrated in Karnataka State (roughly 2,000 miles south of Dharamsala), are now home for more than 19,000 Tibetans; in addition, another 20,000 people have been officially settled in smaller settlements in other parts of the country (*Tibetan Review*, 1976l: 9). Despite the great changes in physical environment and the considerable distance from Himalayan vistas, Tibetans living in the settlements in south India are very successfully maintaining their traditional culture and identity. As M. Goldstein (1975b) points out:

> There has been virtually no assimilation to Indian cultural and social institutions. Concomitantly, there has been the impressive economic adaptation which combines traditional and modern agro-business techniques to exploit successfully the energy potential of a traditional niche. The economic success

of the Tibetans is one of the most striking accomplishments of
the program. (p. 17)

An important aspect of the modern agro-business techniques Goldstein refers to is the cooperative society, whose members include all
settlers above the age of 16. In addition to providing heavy equipment
(tractors and trucks), seed, and fertilizers; running consumer stores
and flour mills; and arranging for the sale of harvested crops, the society also pays the annual rent to the (Indian) state government on
behalf of the settlers. After the harvest, the settlers repay the society
in cash or in kind (*Tibetan Review*, 1977e).

For the children and young people growing up in the settlements,
all this represents at least as much of an education as the formal instruction they receive in the local day school. Once again, in fact,
ideology and experience confront each other. While policies and
rhetoric supporting the practices of elected leadership and communal management might be eagerly promoted by high government officials in Dharamsala, at the local level, cooperation among groups
larger than kinship-linked families does not always occur without
some gentle persuasion from the administration (via lending and re-
payment policies in particular). For young people here, then, opportunities for learning are not limited to such areas as agriculture,
management, or any of the other jobs (employment at the local day
school, handicraft center, machine shop, etc.) available in this setting. In addition, the politics of change also play a significant role in
their experiential education.

To sum up all these post–high school options and activities, let
me briefly review some of the more important lessons taught by
these various life experiences. For those who aspire to continue their
formal education at an Indian institution of higher learning, the
problem of getting financial support is crucial. This in turn puts a
premium on individual initiative, but at the same time, two counter-
ing forces serve to keep personal ambition within socially acceptable
limits. Young people must make their appeal for scholarships in
ways that are not only efficacious but "proper." Furthermore, an intense resentment of favoritism of any type implies a corresponding
emphasis on personal merit as the ideal criterion for determining
grants, awards, and positions of rank.

The young adults enrolled in Tibetan-run institutions are also subject to a variety of new learning experiences. The institute at Sarnath serves as a center of syncretism, a place where old and new philosophical and political ideas and ideologies are debated and considered; the discussions themselves will become part of the intellectual repertoire of the entire Tibetan community. The School of Dialectics, Medical Centre, and Institute of Performing Arts, all located in Dharamsala, not only teach their respective specialties but involve their students, at least indirectly, in a realization of the whole phenomenon of Westerners being interested in Tibetan religion and culture. Global consciousness has also been increased by the drama group's international tour experience, which has served as a two-way mirror for Tibetans and the world to view each other's theatrics.

Young teachers and employees of the Tibetan government, like those engaged in private enterprise, often face conflicting demands stemming from their different and sometimes competing personal and social economic responsibilities. In the end, single-minded devotion to the cause of working for the people usually comes to be somewhat modified by a realistic respect for pragmatic adaptability. Finally, one of the most significant lessons for the entire Tibetan community comes from the experience of the agricultural settlements, where economic success has been linked, ideologically at least, with policies and practices based on elected leadership and communal management. Although this last point is subject to some clarification (i.e., economic endeavors at the local level are still very individualistic [Lawrence Epstein, personal communication]), the general ideal of democratic cooperation is nonetheless being actively promulgated in this context by the programs and rhetoric of the Tibetan government.

Ideas and Ideologies

The ideals and values presented in the Tibetan schools face other counterinfluences besides those that stem from practical economic experience. Young Tibetan thinkers must also confront alternative ideas and ideologies in their intellectual searching, and their struggle to maintain cognitive consistency is further complicated by the shame and despair they and their entire ethnic group feel as a result of having lost their homeland. Such an emotional climate, with its peaks and valleys of idealized national pride as well as bitter disillusionment, might seem to be a very likely environment for demagoguery. In the Tibetan situation, however, this is hardly the case. Those personalities who are most associated with persuasive rhetoric are not demagogues, for rarely is their goal mere self-aggrandizement. Rather, these young leaders, speakers, and writers are engaging in political consciousness raising in the interest of the entire Tibetan community.

The themes of this rhetoric touch both ends of the pride–despair continuum, implying, if not promising, self-respect as a correlative of commitment to a program of Tibetan militancy. The following excerpts from a Tibetan youth publication illustrates this; in passing, it should be noted that the name of the magazine—*March*—refers directly to the key scenario of the Lhasa uprising of March 10, 1959.

> Being a refugee is at best a difficult thing. Being a refugee from Tibet, a land which has for centuries been cut off from the rest of the world, is an extremely traumatic experience. And the hardest-hit victims of this affliction are the young— disoriented, disillusioned and bitter. At that precious moment of youth when life should begin to hold a new and deeper meaning, we the young are confronted with a cynical and indifferent world. . . . The experience "tasting the bitter fruits of defeat" is not a flight of poetic fancy but the accurate description of an extremely unpleasant and intolerable truth. Thus it is that we who once lived proudly in our own land without anybody's help, are now reduced to accepting handouts from the West. . . .
>
> Our position is not an enviable one. A few of us have given up hope and are attempting to gather the shattered fragments of our lives, away from all the bitterness and sorrow, away from our own people. But can we truly escape in this manner? Can we avoid being what we are by merely fleeing from the truth? Never! Flight can never be the answer. For no matter where we flee, we carry with us the blood of our ancestors. It is strong and virile—the same stuff that drove us to transcend our weakness and made us once masters of Central Asia. It is the same stuff that brought the glorious T'ang dynasty of China

ignominiously on its knees—and we have it still. Deep down within each one of us is the same potential. Yet untapped and sluggish after so many years of disuse, but it is there. Thus it is for us to remove all our bitterness and self-pity and to begin exploring our own vitality, assess our strength, analyse our problems and our ideas so that eventually, step by step we may begin to realize our dreams. (*March*, 1976: n.p.)

The second quote is even more specific in its exhortations:

It is high time for the youths to rise and mobilise their potentialities rather than waste it. Let us not recite the particularly empty word Ahimsa [the Buddhist ideal of nonviolence] which has no room in this terrorizing world of today. The policy of Bismarck is the most appropriate one for us to adopt. There is no country in the world who achieved her independence without violence, bloodshed and sacrifice. (*March*, 1976: n.p.)

Such appeals for action, sometimes written and published in English, other times proclaimed aloud at youth meetings in Tibetan, can be seen as the contemporary manifestation of a skill that was traditionally a prerequisite for leadership roles in Tibet: *kha bde-po*, or rhetorical ability. The younger generation, caught between at least two languages and cultures, is consequently less familiar with the fine points of their own rhetorical tradition. Thus today's Tibetan oratory lacks the finesse of the old Tibetan style, which "involved the use of expressive vocabulary within clauses and a sophisticated linking of clauses to express ideas and convey information in subtle, often artistic constructions usually garnished by highly appropriate folk sayings, proverbs and anecdotes" (M. Goldstein, 1968: 132). Contemporary Tibetan writers and speakers have, however, a wide variety of global media at their disposal. At least one Tibetan publication makes use of a worldwide clipping service, and a prominent spokesman for the militant cause recommends popular fiction such as Leon Uris's *Exodus* and *Mila 18* to Tibetan teenagers to inspire their patriotism.

As for the content of the quotations cited above, such unequivocal militancy might be applauded as rhetoric, but it would be wrong to conclude from this that all Tibetans, or even all young Tibetans, would universally support such policies. Nevertheless, such writ-

ings and speeches do serve to influence the political consciousness of the Tibetan community, whose younger members are growing up with a newly cultivated interest in power struggles occurring
throughout the world.

Israel in particular is highly regarded by politically minded Tibetans, for the Jewish diaspora followed by the triumphant reclaim-
ing of a religious homeland appears to them as positive proof that a
tiny but tough nation can ultimately defeat and hold its own against
millions of hostile neighbors. During the week of Tibetan New Year,
an evening social and dance for young people in Dharamsala was ad-
vertised on posters proclaiming the theme: "Next Year in Lhasa!"
Although the dance organizers told me they had never heard of the
corresponding Jewish slogan—"Next Year in Jerusalem"—their explanation could serve just as well to clarify the Passover wish: the
capital, a holy city, is a metonym for the nation. In any case, they
were delighted to learn of this additional parallel between Tibetan
and Jewish experience. Almost all youth leaders have read such
books as Larry Collins and Dominique Lapierre's *O Jerusalem!* and
their interest in the Middle East strongly favors the Israeli point
of view.

The Tibetans' admiration for Israel is virtually unqualified, the
one aspect of Jewish history that invariably does draw unfavorable
comment being the duration of the diaspora ("It shouldn't take us
2,000 years to get *our* country back"). But they are also aware that
the tactics of Israel's enemies have met with success too. Yasser Arafat's gun-wielding entrance into the U.N. General Assembly received much attention in the Tibetan press, and an editorial commenting on this and other such events has itself been quoted and
requoted all over India.

The article sets out to explain the growing militancy of Tibetan
youth, who have "grown up in exile under alien influences, being
thrown aboard and submerged in a sea full of ideas and changes their
parents never experienced before." It then mentions some of the
events in world politics that have particularly affected impression-
able, stateless young refugees:

> They have watched with envy the creation of an independent
> Bangladesh, the consummation of a popular national libera-
> tion struggle in Vietnam, Bhutan's spectacular entry into the

United Nations as an independent nation, and more recently, Yasser Arafat's astonishing success in the United Nations, which seems to vindicate the use of violence or terrorism as an effective instrument of struggle for national rights. (*Tibetan Review*, 1976b: 3)

The most frequently cited lines of this editorial appear sensational when quoted out of context. Taken alone, they seem to be quite simply advocating terrorist tactics:

Apart from the current sound and fury of violence, there has been no actual demonstration of sacrifice for the national cause by any youth. There have been no hijackings, no bomb outrages or spectacular kidnappings. The lamas have done no better. While Buddhist monks in Vietnam or elsewhere immolate themselves for their faith, Tibetan monks in exile seem to abhor the prospects of life after death and content themselves with rituals for a struggle that they hope their gods will fight for them. (*Tibetan Review*, 1976b: 3–4)

Despite the strong, almost bitter tone of these words, the editorial as a whole does not exhort its readers to either violent or nonviolent action but, rather, to collective self-examination. In seeking to account for the failure of Tibetan resistance movements, it examines the unique sacral-political form of Tibetan leadership and finds there a tragic irony: such a dually oriented institution is "an asset for peaceful means" (of accommodating to present realities), but it is also "a liability for an armed struggle" (*Tibetan Review*, 1976b: 4).

The editorial goes on to explore the implications of this ambiguity, pointing out both the benefits that have accrued to Tibetan refugees as a result of the Dalai Lama's international stature as a religious leader and the disadvantages that stem from this "preponderantly spiritual" mode of leadership: "the conspicuous lack of progress in their armed struggle for independence." The crux of the problem here concerns the unique institutionalized sacrality of the Dalai Lama. Once legitimated as the authentic reincarnation of Avalokiteshvara, this figure is regarded by Tibetans as being personally above what Balandier (1972/1967) has termed "impure, violent contestations for power" (pp. 99–122). Yet militant Tibetans, acutely conscious of their need for a leader who would rule "by steel and blood"

(p. 7), must look in vain for the Tibetan equivalent of a Ho Chi Minh, a Che Guevera, or a Sheikh Mujib, for

> it is impossible for any other leader, secular or otherwise, to replace or even challenge the Dalai Lama's leadership as long as he lives. This is not because he wants to perpetuate his "rule" like other worldly politicians, but because of the five centuries of "papal" authority and aura surrounding the name of the Dalai Lama. . . . All this makes any alternative to the leadership impossible and adds a tragic inevitability to the Tibetan drama. (p. 4)

Attempts to come to terms with this cognitive-ideological impasse can be noted in the intellectual and symbolic expressions that are being formulated and elaborated by Tibetan refugees today. Three general types of ideological strategies can be identified. First, young people who took their religion for granted in elementary and secondary school are now turning to a less devotional, more intellectual study of Buddhism, seeking to find there precedents and justifications for violence as well as areas of rapprochement between this religious thought system and other more secular and political ideologies such as Marxism, socialism, and communism. Second, many of the most radical youths have adopted a neopuritanical attitude characterized by an intense single-mindedness of purpose and a fierce intolerance for other Tibetans' complacency or opportunism. Far from wishing to desacralize the "pure, just, and organizing" character of their leader's legitimacy, these concerned young monitors of "proper" symbolization speak out strongly and often against any perceived disrespect to the Dalai Lama or Western-influenced commercialization of their religion. Third, the word *rangzen*, as explained in the first chapter of this book, can refer to a significantly broader range of referents than its translation as "independence" might indicate. In fact, the more far-reaching connotations of this twentieth-century neologism make it a particularly apt vehicle for conveying a whole set of attitudes and strategies that Tibetans associate with the concept of freedom; and this multivocalic potential is definitely, though not always consciously, being exploited by Tibetans from all walks of life. Let me now explore each of these three strategies in more detail, paying particular attention to the interaction between traditional, familiar ideology and current, alien sociopolitical experience.

The fact that many young Tibetans are now attempting to reexamine their religion with more sophisticated questions in mind does not, in itself, represent a radical break with tradition, for Buddhism has always been able to accommodate a wide variety of rational and critical-minded believers. What is new about the present case, however, is the direct influence of earlier schooling on this first refugee generation of Tibetan young adults. Having been exposed to a modern education, complete with large and deliberate doses of Western science and rationalism, the more thoughtful youth are now experiencing what a close friend of mine described as "psychological anguish." As he saw it, the vast majority of Tibetans in the past believed in their religion uncritically, "with a blind faith." Now that is no longer possible, especially for those who feel a strong personal need to integrate old traditions with new ways of thought. Yet as my friend put it, "the mere realization that some beliefs and practices were absurd solves nothing. I have to decide what to accept and what to reject with my own brain. I want to preserve my culture, but I have also learned to question."

In his book, Dawa Norbu (1974) relates an incident form his own life that illustrates the same problem. Eight years after his escape to India, he was a scholarship student at an Anglo-Indian school in Kalimpong.

> My class was doing *Twelfth Night*. The clown, disguised as a curate, asks Malvolio: "What is the opinion of Pythagoras concerning wild fowl?" Malvolio from the dark house replies: "That the soul of our grandam might haply inhabit a bird." The whole class roared with laughter. I joined in half-heartedly. I was neither as negative as my class-mates, including the teacher, who thought that the theory of rebirth was a joke; nor was I as positive as my mother, who felt that rebirth was as certain as the certitude of death. Ever since then I have been seeking explanations. (p. 52)

This search for intellectual integrity is being pursued with specific directedness by a small, serious-minded group of students at the Central Institute of Higher Tibetan Studies described in the first section of this chapter. The principal of this institution is a remarkable man on many counts. He is young but a recognized scholar according to traditional standards, having completed his Geshe Lharampa degree, roughly equivalent to a Ph.D. in Buddhist philosophy, in 1968/1969. He has also acquired considerable expertise in both the theory and the praxis of contemporary Indian politics. In an interview he told me how deeply disturbed he had been when he first heard the Dalai Lama speaking in praise of certain positive aspects of Marxism and communism. Like most other Tibetans of that time (before 1970), his political views were then, if anything, anti-communist.[5] Thus, as he explained it, "I was very much perturbed, for I could neither deny His Holiness' words nor could I accept his praising of communism and Marxism. Later I studied more and came to know more facts. My views got changed. Similarly, the views of many students here have also changed."

The year 1970 in fact marks the date of the All-India Seminar on Marxism and Buddhism, which was held at this institute and personally attended by the Dalai Lama. The next year, the institute hosted a second meeting of this type, this one on the social philosophy of Buddhism. Ideas presented and discussed at both gatherings shared the general theme of social dynamics, particularly the dialectical interaction between religious-philosophical principles and actual temporal problems, while giving specific consideration to relevant issues in Indian and Tibetan history (problems of caste and warfare, respectively).

At the 1971 seminar, the then newly appointed principal of the institute read his paper "The Social and Political Strata in Buddhist

5. Despite the Dalai Lama's occasional statements supporting certain aspects of communist and Marxist theory, the vast majority of Tibetans still do regard communism as a dangerous if not morally reprehensible ideology. On May 1, 1979, three young Tibetans (two college graduates and a former security guard in Chinese-ruled Tibet who only left Tibet in 1974) formally announced the formation of the Tibetan Communist party of the Tibetans in exile. Reaction from the Tibetan community was swift and extremely negative. In particular, much criticism focused on the statement in the party's manifesto that "every member has the freedom to practice and the freedom not to practice religion" (*Tibetan Review*, 1980b: 8).

On March 10, 1982, the three executives of the party (who were, in fact, its original founders) announced that the party had been disbanded because of an acute lack of financial support and because "petty and unending surveillance and harassment" by "class enemies" made normal functioning of their organization impossible (*Tibetan Review*, 1982b).

Thought," which has since been reprinted in two different Tibetan publications. Included in this presentation is a discussion of the principles that should govern a defensive war; furthermore, it is this paper that cites the Jataka story of Sarthavaha Sattvavana, which has become the standard ideological justification for violence among militant Tibetan youth.

The story concerns a wicked ferryman who was about to murder and rob the passengers on his vessel. The Buddha, who was also on board in the form of the bodhisattva Sarthavaha Sattvavana, was moved by compassion for both the passengers and the criminal; thus motivated, he slew the ferryman "to save him from the great sinful act which he planned to perform, by which he would incur the consequences of the sinful deed" (Samdong Rinpoche, 1977: 2).

This particular story was quoted to me every time I talked with young, militant Tibetans on the subject of politically motivated violence. In fact, their sensitivity to its symbolic potential was much more acute than mine here. In response to my question of why Dpal-gyi rdo-rje (the ninth-century monk who killed the king's assassin) was not cited more often as a precedent for suspending *ahimsa* (the Buddhist ideal of nonviolence), I was told that that particular incident was indeed relevant, but the Jataka story had the Buddha himself, and not just a mere man, performing the action.

I have heard similar justifications for violence from young people who initially appeared to me as having little else in common. A shy young poet who had been a guerilla fighter in Mustang (Nepal) several years earlier told me that *"ahimsa* has to be temporarily put aside because in Tibet today religion is being attacked and demolished." An irrepressible young monk who has been jailed for engaging in political demonstrations in the Lok Sabha (Indian Parliament) explained his militant participation in this way: "My family has traditionally been involved in religion as well as politics; in fact, as a monk I feel I'm even more free to devote myself to the cause than a layman with family responsibilities. As for violence, there is a Jataka story with this message: 'Better one should die than many.'"

Finally, the same kind of intellectual manipulation can be seen in an editorial from *Rangzen* (1977), which interprets the Buddhist doctrine of the Middle Path in this way: "It is in this instance the Middle Path between the virtual suicide of pacifistic complacency and the unjustifiable aggression against the weak" (p. 2). The article concludes by seeing in Buddhism a kind of situation ethics that can ultimately be linked with a traditional Tibetan aphorism supporting a holy war:

> The strength of Buddhism lies in the fact that it takes into account the fact that the problems in life are far too complex and contradictory to be instantly solved by a set of rigid ethical codes.
>
> Thus Buddhism exposes the hollowness of modern pacifism and other similar naive ideas. Instead it directs us to the wisdom and common sense of our ancestors who coined this saying:
> For the Buddha faced by foemen
> His disciples don their armour. (p. 3)

The counterpart to this strongly expressed regard for violent, contesting power can be seen in the corresponding idealization of the pure and just aspects of Tibetan tradition, beliefs, and values. It is in this root sense that the term *neopuritanism* may be used to characterize these tendencies and attitudes, for adherents of this point of view are resolutely intolerant of any perceived corruption in the mentality and practices of their own people—and those of outsiders too—whenever such behavior impinges disrespectfully, in their view, on Tibetan sacred–profane boundaries.

Foremost among neopuritan concerns is the maintenance of proper awe and respect for the sanctity of the key summarizing symbol, the Dalai Lama. As a leader in the Tibetan youth movement explained to me, "I'm different from you. I have a sense of identification with His Holiness—a link so strong it continues past death into the next life. That's why we can't tolerate *any* sort of criticism of His Holiness. He is the symbol of a lot of things we aspire to." He also expressed the deep shame he feels upon seeing the stream of all-too-casual Westerners coming to Dharamsala to have an audience with the Dalai Lama:

> Every two-bit freak goes to ask His Holiness weird questions. And sometimes you feel bad. They would have a harder time trying to meet President Carter, but it's easy for them just to talk to His Holiness and ask questions. I don't mind if people

really talk to His Holiness, but there's something important there. I prefer Indians meeting His Holiness. They never ask very many questions. They just go there and get *darshan;* you know, Indians feel this sense of blessing in the presence of a holy man. We try to do the same. We try never to abuse this privilege when we see His Holiness.

Yet Tibetans' supreme respect for their leader is never so totally transcendence oriented as to preclude their very real need for a flesh-and-blood symbol. As I explained in the first chapter, the Tibetan community was deeply distressed by the rumor in 1976 that "the Dalai Lama may not be in our midst any longer." The reaction of young college students and graduates as well as simple, unlettered old people was the same: "His Holiness *cannot* end the line of reincarnations. He is the only symbol that unites us all. We *need* his continued presence among us."

This fervent desire to preserve the supreme Tibetan institution unchanged has its counterpart, among the neopuritans, in their outspoken criticism of a trend they see as deplorable: the cheapening and commercialization of traditional cultural expressions. An editorial in *Rangzen* (1976a) begins with this observation:

> *Bco-lnga mchod-pa* or "The Offering of the Fifteenth" is a serenely beautiful festival when the monks of the Tantric College of Lhasa display fascinating examples of butter sculptures, fourteen days after the Tibetan New Year. Last year a sad note crept into this occasion. The festival was illuminated with numerous and garish Christmas lights blinking off and on, casting the harsh shadows of Las Vegas and Reno on the delicate features of our gentle Buddhist deities. Is this our culture? (p. 2)

The article goes on to point out other examples of "bad taste," "diluted Buddhism," and "bastardized" cultural forms: sacred images put out for unrestricted sale in the now-lucrative "dharma market"; Tibetan lamas going abroad to join the "guru racket" instead of teaching their own people first; and in a nonreligious vein, a style of speech that is "riddled with unnecessary English phrases and Hindi words" (p. 5).

Other items in the Tibetan press mirror this concern. Articles on dharma courses for Westerners in Dharamsala (*Tibetan Review*, 1972a) and Tibetan Buddhism in the West (*Tibetan Review*, 1979: 3–4; 22–23); an interview with a Western specialist on Buddhism (*Tibetan Review*, 1975); and a cautionary note on "adopting Dharma to American conditions" (*Tibetan Review*, 1976n) all document the fears of even the most mildly neopuritanical Tibetans that their "pure" tradition, which has for centuries idealized the image of the solitary saint meditating in the mountains, is in danger of being replaced by a grotesque caricature that would evaluate a religious teacher's "success" according to the appeal of his "show business."

The two general intellectual and symbolic strategies I have discussed so far—the politically motivated study of Buddhism and the neopuritanical war on corruption and opportunism—complement each other by balancing the demand for violence and militancy with a corresponding concern for preserving intact the most "pure" and "just" aspects of Tibetan tradition. (In passing, one notes how this pattern replicates a characteristic feature of Tibetan iconography: the standard acknowledgment of two contrasting forms, a "wrathful" [*drag-po*] and a "peaceful" [*zhi-ba*] aspect, for one and the same deity.) A similar ambiguity can also be detected in the words, actions, and symbolism of the Dalai Lama (see Gupta, 1973). He is both a political and a nonpolitical leader, and he speaks of going back to Tibet yet heads a government-in-exile that pursues policies clearly geared to continued Tibetan residence in India. Furthermore, his "transcendent" aspect, which links him with the bodhisattva of compassion, is balanced by an "immanence" that associates him with international power struggles.

A third symbolic strategy Tibetans may employ in their attempts to make sense of conflicting ideas and ideologies is likewise based on polysemy. In this case, however, the possibilities of interpretation are not so much oppositions that counter each other in a neither-nor, either-or pattern; rather, they are broadly multivalent. As I have explained, the word *rangzen* is replete with semantic as well as historical connotative possibilities. Whether taken in the literal sense of the Tibetan morphemes *rang* ("self") and *btsan* ("power") or interpreted metaphorically as a metapolitical image of independence, this concept directly impinges on two of the most critical problems Tibetan refugees must confront today: that of *self*-definition (either as individuals vis-à-vis others, especially Tibetans, or as Tibetans vis-à-vis the rest of the world) and that of de facto and de jure relationships of *power* (again, in reference to both intra-Tibetan and Tibetan–non-Tibetan sociopolitical relationships).

By virtue of this evocative potency, the *rangzen* metaphor is simultaneously able to draw on, as well as enrich, the stock of traditional Tibetan feelings and ideas. The behavioral ideal of *ya-rabs spyod-bzang* ("respectful" or "proper" behavior), for example, is culturally reinforced by a socialization process that heightens Tibetans' sensitivity to *ngo-tsha* ("shame" or "face" consciousness; literally, "hot face"), which would, of course, be avoided at all costs in any "proper" interpersonal relationship. This concern for "the other" has its dialectic counterpart in the special attention paid to the "self," whether this be an individual "I" or a collective "we." In either case, it is not just failure or wrongdoing that is to be avoided, but even more important, public humiliation. A striking acknowledgment of this kind of "face" consciousness can be noted in the following words of a Tibetan youth leader:

> When you become a refugee, you lose dignity because you've lost the land. You feel shame: His Holiness has been kicked out of his own country when you know there's no better leader in the world. Sometimes you feel so mad—ashamed of your own people just sitting there doing nothing [for independence]. That's why I admire people like the Japanese, who, if they can't do it, they commit *hara-kiri*. It's a positive thing. It's showing that you can't bear the shame any more.

The conventional interpretation of *rangzen* does, in fact, support, as well as draw strength from, this set of behavioral ideals: "proper" behavior, "face" consciousness, and patriotism (*rgyal-zhen*). In other words, by achieving independence in the political sense, Tibetans would vindicate their shame at having lost their country. But in addition to these sociopolitical elaborations, the notion of *rangzen* is also being creatively manipulated around the religious ideal of *snying-rje* ("compassion"). The way in which this supreme value of Tibetan Buddhism is being linked with independence involves a subtle intertwining of both domains of meaning: traditional religious associations as well as contemporary political themes.

In my conversations with the most politically active Tibetan young people, I would often hear them criticize certain devotional practices they considered "excessive" or "too much for show" (e.g., "the waste of all that butter" for votive lamps, or *phyag-'tshal* [prostrations before sacred images] "done only to impress others"). I then began asking a simple question: What *is* sacred to you then? Without a moment's hesitation the answer would come back (unanimously, from this group at least): "*Rangzen!*" A university student clarified this somewhat: "Not just independence, but freedom in an intangible sense." Another young man elaborated this still further: "We are fighting for freedom in the very highest sense—the freedom to reach Nirvana."

This explanation is extremely significant. It effectively sacralizes the goal of *rangzen* by broadening the political concept of freedom to the point of utter (religious) transcendence, or Nirvana. This association can be even further elaborated. The youth leader I quoted earlier told me that "Tibet produced saints the way Ford produces cars." He, and others too, specifically mentioned Milarepa, the mischievously joyful ascetic who glorified both nature and the supernatural in poetry and song, as the primary example of what "a free Tibet could offer to the whole world." Milarepa, who lived in the twelfth century, and whose style in some ways resembles that of Francis of Assisi in Christian tradition, is regarded by all Tibetans as a saint, in fact, as the beloved prototype of the most highly esteemed Tibetan figure of all: the hermit meditating in the mountains "for the benefit of all sentient beings." "If Tibet were free," goes the argument, "the whole world could profit by the religious activities of such spiritual giants." *Rangzen* would thus permit all sentient creatures to share in Tibet's special glory: saints who, by definition, are compassionate.

In summary, then, new connotations are now accumulating around the orthodox meanings of the values emphasized so strongly in the Tibetan schools: compassion (*snying-rje*), respectful behavior (*ya-rabs spyod-bzang*), patriotism (*rgyal-zhen*), and avoiding shame (*ngo-tsha*). This cumulative process is, in turn, nourished by the growing complexity of sociopolitical contingencies and cultural ideals now confronting Tibetan young adults. Current political events throughout the world—in particular, the struggles of other stateless peoples for jural recognition—likewise play a major role in influencing many young Tibetans' views about another exceedingly important issue: the efficacy of violent as opposed to nonviolent means of achieving a national goal of independence. At the same time, however, the sacredness of the Dalai Lama, the supreme Tibetan authority figure and summarizing symbol, would be compromised for Tibetans were he ever to appear unequivocally as a militaristic leader: thus it is extremely unlikely that an explicitly pro-violence policy could ever again gain the unambiguous support of the entire Tibetan community.

Nonetheless, Tibetans are making intellectual and symbolic attempts to come to terms with this impasse, and these attempts can be described in terms of three general strategies: (1) a less devotional, more politically motivated reconsideration of Buddhist tradition; (2) a neopuritanical concern for maintaining the purity of essential Tibetan symbolic forms; and (3) a sometimes conventional, sometimes extended interpretation of the metapolitical concept of *rangzen*. At the intellectual level, at least, Tibetans can and do employ and manipulate this notion to help stabilize the seesawing tensions between religious faith and rational doubt; sacred and secular power; violence and nonviolence; avoiding shame and promoting compassion. In fact, all the ideas and ideologies discussed in this section can be translated by this metaphor into a comprehensive, more or less coherent, and experientially relevant model of and for action: working to achieve independence.

The Politics of Youth

Before I explore the dramatized counterpart of this metaphor—the key scenario of the annual March 10 commemoration—let me first describe the political context of these two evolving symbols, particularly with respect to the focus of this study, Tibetan youth. Obviously, a thorough examination of this topic could easily become a study in its own right; thus I limit the scope here to providing relevant background information rather than a complete description of contemporary Tibetan politics. This established, let me turn to the implications of two general types of confrontation Tibetan youth are experiencing today: that between old- and new-style politics within the Tibetan community and that between the group as a whole and the world at large vis-à-vis "the cause of Tibet."

In the first case, both the officials of the Tibetan government-in-exile and the Tibetan population in general are being affected by the growing trend of democratization in Tibetan sociopolitical institutions. The "Constitution of Tibet" (1963), formulated over the 3-year period 1960–1963, was promulgated by the Dalai Lama on March 10, 1963. In the foreward to this bilingually published document, His Holiness explains the conditions of its inception:

> Even prior to my departure from Tibet in March, 1959, I had come to the conclusion that in the changing circumstances of the modern world the system of governance in Tibet must be so modified and amended as to allow the elected representatives of the people to play a more effective role in guiding and shaping the social and economic policies of the State. (p. v)

In addition to providing for democratic representation, however, the Constitution also continues the traditional and explicit Tibetan affirmation of *chos-srid zung-'brel*, the domain of "the religious and the political combined":

> This Constitution . . . takes into consideration the doctrines enunciated by Lord Buddha, the spiritual and temporal heritage of Tibet, and the ideas and ideals of the modern world. It is thus intended to secure for the people of Tibet a system of democracy based on justice and equality and ensure their cultural, religious and economic development. (p. v)

This clearly acknowledged attempt to come to terms with both worlds—the spiritual and the temporal or, alternatively, the traditional (familiar) and the modern (alien)—can be seen in other aspects of contemporary Tibetan polity as well. The implementation of the Constitution is regarded by Tibetans as "still provisional" because "it can only be finalized after consulting the wishes of all Tibetan people, and this can only be done when we are able to go back to Tibet" (*Tibetans in Exile*, 1969: 315). Nevertheless, since 1960 Tibetan refugees over 18 years of age have been electing delegates every 3 years to serve in the legislative branch of their government-in-exile. In this connection there is another attempt to accommodate past attitudes into a new political framework; regional and sectarian affiliations are not only recognized but actually built right into the system.

The first elections were held to fill 13 positions: three members from each of the three major regions of Tibet (Dbus-Gtsang: central, southern, and western Tibet; Amdo: northeastern Tibet; and Khams: eastern Tibet), to be chosen by lay people originally from those areas; and one member from each of the four main Tibetan Buddhist sects (Rnying-ma-pa; Sa-skya-pa; Bka'-rgyud-pa; and Dge-lugs-pa), to be selected by religious of the corresponding order. This group of officials constituting the Commission of Tibetan People's Deputies (renamed the Assembly of Tibetan Peoples Deputies in 1980) represents the top level in the administrative hierarchy of the legislative branch of the Tibetan government.[6] Its function is ideally conceived of as exercising a check on the executive branch—the Kashag (*bka'-shag*), or Cabinet of Ministers—which is composed of the secretaries (directors) of the six administrative departments: the Council of Religious and Cultural Affairs; the Office of Home Affairs; the Security Office; the Office of Service and Management (formerly combined with the previous department and then known as the Security and Personnel Office); the Council for Tibetan Education; and the Information and Publicity Office. (In December 1981, the Department of Health was also added.)

This group of appointed officials and their staffs make up what is known as the Tibetan Secretariat: an expansive network of ranked positions that are still correlated with traditional honorific titles, even though access to these posts is now open to all. Together with the elected representatives of the Commission of the Tibetan People's Deputies, these members of the Tibetan government are known collectively (and with the usual connotations) as "the Dharamsala establishment," a political hierarchy that receives de facto recognition from all Tibetans in exile.

Despite this basic acknowledgment of legitimacy, made concrete in the form of a "voluntary" tax paid annually by Tibetans both in India and abroad, the government has its share of Tibetan critics as well. In addition to the usual kinds of contention that might occur in any government setting with respect to personalities, vested interests, and so forth, a significant new factor is entering into much of the antiestablishment criticism the institution receives. Young and old Tibetans alike are learning more and more about democracy, both in theory and in practice. The new Constitution (1963) guar-

---

6. For a description of local-level administration positions, see M. Goldstein (1975b: 19). For evolution of the electoral system, see the Appendix to this volume.

antees equality regardless of "sex, race, language, religion, social origin, property, birth or other status" (chap. II, article 8). School children are being indoctrinated with a new ideology, which puts national, group consciousness above regional and sectarian loyalties. Finally, some of the statements made by the most recent refugees from Tibet are also affecting the development of Tibetan political consciousness.

A Tibetan woman who arrived in India in 1974 has written a book (translated by the Information and Publicity Office into English) about her experience under the Chinese regime. Her words, and others like them, are becoming more commonly heard, repeated, and discussed throughout the Tibetan community today: "Though the Chinese indoctrinations do not make me an atheist, I still think that Communism has a lot of practical lessons for the Tibetans. In the old days when Tibet was independent, religion became increasingly dominated by temporal things like power, wealth and rank—instead of compassion" (Dhondup Choedon, 1978: 70).

With such ideas becoming more widely known and discussed by all segments of the Tibetan population, it is no wonder that certain policies—those suspected of at least tacitly supporting old strongholds of inequality—are coming due for more criticism than ever before. A Tibetan researcher (Samten G. Karmay, 1977a) who has lived and studied in London, Paris, and Tokyo has written a rather tendentious essay decrying the role played by sectarian feuds throughout Tibetan history. In addition to discussing past problems of this nature, he also shows how the same policies are being continued today, still to the detriment of Tibetan unity.

> The present trend of Tibetan activities in setting up meditational centres in the U.S. and Europe is good as far as it goes. It may be providing much needed spiritual healing for the mentally tired people of a materialistic world. However, there is nothing new in this movement. Far from it, it is a logical extension of the old sectarian interests seeking foreign patronage. The sectarian bias is not only thus maintained, but also imparted to those faithful western followers who naturally feel that it is their duty to uphold such differences. (p. 26)

Another young Tibetan (K. Dhondup, 1977a), an employee of the Library of Tibetan Works and Archives in Dharamsala, has made similar protests, first against sectarianism, which he sees as "still a very living disease in the exile Tibetan society" (p. 34), and then against the policy by which delegates are still elected to the Commission of Tibetan People's Deputies according to regional and sectarian affiliation (K. Dhondup, 1977b; see also Appendix). What he has suggested to replace this system is a new policy by which delegates would be elected "on the basis of the population strength of Tibetan settlements, camps and other areas where Tibetans live" (p. 30). Furthermore, he would like election campaigns to be introduced so that the voting public may be educated to select politically conscientious representatives rather than "rimpoches, tulkus [*sprul-sku*, or incarnate lamas] and sons and daughters of high and rich families (p. 30)."

These and similar comments and criticisms are spoken, written, and promulgated quite freely in the Tibetan community, but their actual effect on official government is quite minimal. Because Tibetans still regard the Dalai Lama as their supreme ruler both religiously and politically, no antigovernment protests have ever gained sufficient momentum to present a real challenge to the establishment, which is adept at intimating that dissent against the government could amount to sacrilege against its sacred symbol.

Despite (or perhaps more accurately, because of) this traditional, built-in guarantee of the status quo, certain alternative political groups have not only been tolerated but even to some degree actively encouraged by the Tibetan government. In October 1970 a conference was held in Dharamsala for Tibetan youth from all over India. At that 8-day meeting, which strongly emphasized the common bond of religious, cultural, and national identity, the Dalai Lama himself addressed the assemblage, speaking one day on Buddhism and the future of Tibet and concluding the conference on the last day with these thoughts:

> Having held this youth conference during the past few days, let us ask ourselves what is the most essential task for the young people. The answer is: service to the people. In order to serve the people one must learn the difficulties and the sufferings of the people by keeping close touch with them. Similarly, you cannot lead the people if you lose touch with them.
> (Quoted in *Tibetan Review*, 1970: 7)

As a result of this meeting, a permanent organization, the Tibetan Youth Congress (TYC) was created. With headquarters in Dharamsala, it had, at the time of my fieldwork, over 5,000 members in 28 different regions in India and abroad. There is no upper limit on age; young people start to attend local meetings and officially join in high school. While many activities of the TYC at the local level are oriented toward service to the Tibetan community (e.g., adult literacy programs, hygiene education, help with filling out registration forms, interpreting, etc.), the stated goal of the group is much more political and all-embracing: "The avowed aim of the Tibetan Youth Congress is the creation of a free and independent Tibet and the restoration of His Holiness the Dalai Lama to his rightful position as the sole religious and temporal leader of all Tibet" (standard back page of *Rangzen*, the bilingual magazine published by the TYC).

Given the profound affective importance of this goal, those who speak out on its behalf are by and large assured of Tibetan support of their speechmaking; thus the often-militant rhetoric of TYC leaders is generally accepted, or at least unchecked by the establishment, so long as it is directed toward the international situation and not against the government-in-exile. Nonetheless, criticism against the latter organization does occur, and not infrequently. The young, who see less and less hope for the efficacy of subtle, indirect, and cautious strategies, are beginning to express their strong impatience with and disapproval of present priorities. The Dharamsala establishment was particularly stung by an article in *Rangzen* that accused it of being little more than "a giant charitable organization rather than an effective machinery designed to fight for the rights of a nation" (Lodi Gyaltsen Gyari, 1976: 7).

In fact, the issue of verbal disputation is important in this connection in its own right. TYC leaders are proud of the free and open way their meetings are conducted. As one official of the Central Executive Committee told me, "If someone talks rubbish, we put him down immediately. We want results, not old-style respect." But at the regional level, away from the sometimes heady atmosphere of Dharamsala the "capital," there is some disillusionment among the more reflective youth: "What has the TYC ever done for independence besides fight a war with words?"

This phrase—"a war with words"—is indeed a telling one. Despite all the self-proclaimed differences between the quasi-militant TYC and its parent figure, the Tibetan government itself, the actual activities of both groups vis-à-vis "the cause of Tibet" have in most cases been quite similar except for the contrast in verbal style. Both organizations have gone on record affirming the spiritual and temporal leadership of the Dalai Lama, demanding a supervised plebiscite in Tibet, and recommending that petitions be sent to the United Nations, urging that body to implement resolutions it passed in 1959, 1961, and 1965 calling for the restoration of human rights in Tibet. Since the time of my fieldwork, however, a substantial disagreement between the two groups has emerged regarding the Tibetan government's sponsorship of four official delegations to Tibet. According to *Tibetan Review* (1980d), "the TYC has concluded that Peking is only interested in luring the Dalai Lama back to Tibet and put him under house arrest, and to solve the border dispute with India without fear of Tibetan intervention" (p. 5).

The preeminence of the Tibetan government over subsidiary Tibetan political organizations can be seen even more obviously in the case of two other alternative Tibetan movements that, unlike the TYC, arose independently of the establishment. In the first instance —that of the Movement for the Restoration of Tibet's Rightful Independence (*bod rang-dbang bden-pa'i slar-gso'i las-'gul*)—a conference "organized and attended entirely by the masses" first convened in July 1972 following a statement by India's external affairs minister that "Tibet is a part of China." As a result of this meeting, Tibetan college and university students postponed their annual examinations and dispersed throughout India to educate and mobilize the Tibetan community regarding the need for, and the tactics of, the new independence movement. At the conclusion of the conference, however, "it was agreed that the leadership of the movement would henceforth be taken over by the Commission of the Tibetan People's Deputies" (*Tibetan Review*, 1972b: 5). From that point on, the pattern of "war with words" was once again fixed. The outcome of subsequent meetings—in October 1973 and in March 1976—was basically verbal. As a result of the second conference, "a strong reminder" was submitted to the U.N. secretary general regarding implementation of the three resolutions the United Nations had previously passed supporting human rights in Tibet. The third meeting ended similarly: yet another petition sent to the United Nations.

The second grass-roots organization, the Tibetan People's Freedom Movement, met a different fate. Its leaders, the Coordinating Committee, reluctantly agreed to the demands of the Tibetan government that they disband. The short-lived history of the leadership of this most recent popularly formed body is particularly relevant to the March 10 commemoration, for it was in connection with this demonstration in Delhi in 1977 that the Tibetan People's Freedom Movement came into being.

Some of the circumstances of this episode were influenced by sheer coincidence: the recent relaxing of the Indian Emergency, the stunning upset of Indira Gandhi in the national elections, and the coming to power of the Janata party, whose leaders had been outspoken defenders of Tibetan rights for the past two decades. Other, doubly significant elements of this symbolic drama (Tibetan volunteers, acutely conscious of national "face," on a "hunger strike unto death"; newly elected officials of the Janata party bringing them fruit juice, an unprepared but "pure" food, to break their fast 10 days later) were certainly not without precedent in the context in which this all occurred: twentieth-century India, three decades after Mahatma Gandhi's passive resistance against the British.

What happened, in brief, was this. Anticipating the annual March 10 demonstration, the Indian authorities published on March 8 a ban on public meetings and processions in the Chanakyapuri area of New Delhi, where the Chinese and other embassies are located. On March 10, ignoring the ban, six busloads of Tibetans began proceeding from their early morning meeting place—a Tibetan Buddhist temple near a large Tibetan camp—to the site of the embassy. When they arrived there, a cordon of police was already waiting for them. A disturbance broke out between the two groups over the Tibetans' insistence that a memorandum be delivered to the Chinese, who were watching all this behind the embassy wall. As a result of the ensuing melee, 209 Tibetans, including 53 women and an unspecified number of children, were arrested and jailed for 2 days (*Tibetan Review*, 1977d: 7).

According to a participant, a high school boy from my fieldwork site, the jail experience was one of exceptional *communitas*, to use Turner's term. What little food, tobacco, and matches the group possessed was generously shared: "We were like one big family." It was in this atmosphere that the idea of a hunger strike was first suggested, some say by the women, who were jailed separately. The proposal was viewed as a possible means of forcing the Indian authorities to deliver the ill-fated memorandum to the Chinese, which never happened. In any case, after 2 days in jail, the entire group was released on bail. Hundreds of other Tibetans who had not been arrested were waiting for them—and also for a new plan of action. From this situation, which resulted in a spontaneously mobilized group, the Tibetan People's Freedom Movement was born.

This extremely purposeful gathering of Tibetans, headed by leaders who just happened to be there (representatives of the various local Tibetan communities who had come to Delhi to be part of the March 10 demonstration), decided to channel the tremendous sense of excitement and hope that had been generated by the experience. Meetings were held, and 83 Tibetans volunteered to go on a hunger strike "unto death." The plan called for an initial group of 7 volunteers, who would be replaced one by one as soon as an individual would die. On March 20 at 10:00 A.M., the first group—6 men and 1 woman—sat cross-legged on a raised platform outside the U.N. Information Centre, resolutely determined to die slowly and publicly if their demands for U.N. action on the Tibet resolutions were not met. The following is an excerpt from a press release explaining their position.

> We Tibetans are treated as political lepers by the international community and our cause as an embarrassing and contagious disease. We the victims are ignored and shunted while our oppressors are courted and feted by a world gone mad.
>
> We are a peaceful people and we have nowhere to turn to for justice except the United Nations. We do not ask for charity. We only demand what is ours, what was assured to us by the U.N. in its three resolutions. The United Nations in those days claimed impotence, as Red China was not a member of that international body. But now Red China is not only a member, but also sits in the Security Council. Hence, we urge the United Nations to implement your resolutions passed on Tibet.

The first significant but unplanned event to impinge on the hunger strike occurred early March 21, when returns from the 3-day Indian national election showed quite conclusively that the "impossible" had indeed happened and Indira Ghandi would no longer be prime minister. In this atmosphere, where even regular (Indian) Congress party supporters were exultant over what they saw as the triumph of Indian democracy over authoritarianism, Tibetans themselves became hopeful about the implications for their own cause. In fact, the initial omens looked very good indeed.

On March 28 the general secretary of the Janata party, Surendra Mohan, wrote a letter to the hunger strikers asking them to discontinue their fast and included with the letter the text of a telegram his party had sent to the United Nations: "Strongly urge immediate implementation United Nations resolutions on Tibet." On March 30 other Janata party notables (George Fernandes, the fiery opposition leader who had himself been jailed during the Emergency; Raj Narayan, another newly appointed cabinet minister; and the party's grand old man Acharya J. B. Kripalani, who in fact was the person to offer the orange juice to the fasting volunteers) also appeared at the site of the fast, made speeches defending Tibetan rights, and personally requested the seven volunteers to end their fast. This public and very sensitively managed affirmation of Tibetan "face" by the Janata leaders was backed up on the Tibetan side by a message from the Dalai Lama, also asking the group to break their fast. Encouraged by all these indications of support and solidarity, they did so at 12:55 P.M. on March 30. The statement they released on the occasion shows that their action, too, was very much motivated by a concern for proper "face" relations:

> The Janata Party having reassured us of their unequivocal support, have asked us to withdraw our fast. Some of its prominent leaders, Mr. Surendra Mohan, Mr. George Fernandes, and especially Acharya Kripalani are here today to ask us not to carry on. It would be ungrateful in the face of all this sympathy and support to refuse. Furthermore, we have no desire whatsoever to embarrass the New Janata Government and the nation.

But their statement also contains this acknowledgment of Tibetan disillusionment with "the rest of the world":

> The total silence maintained by the Secretary General of the U.N. has led us to regretfully conclude that the U.N. is no more than a facade for the hypocrisy of the big powers, and its

Charter, noble as it may sound, is not worth the paper it is written on. We are simple people and we believe that speech and action should go hand and hand.

This reaction of disillusionment was typical of the thoughts expressed by Tibetans for weeks afterward. Especially for the younger members of the community (junior and senior high school students), who had been following the events of the hunger strike with intense interest and concern, the harsh realities of international realpolitik came as a painful shock. Brought up to attach great value to respect, propriety, and good intentions, their initial hopes about the superpowers aiding the Tibetan cause were not only unrealistic in the extreme but poignant as well. Thus a high school boy wrote a letter to the editor in which, with almost painful sincerity, he urged all Tibetans to write to President Carter about human rights in Tibet: "When such petitions are made in a lawful and proper manner by all Tibetans who are in a position to do so, we feel certain that the conscience of the leaders of these great nations will be moved to take into consideration our just appeal" (Pasang Dhondup, 1977).

As for the ultimate denouement of the Tibetan People's Freedom Movement, this too, brought disillusionment to those who had hoped too much. After the termination of the hunger strike, the seven volunteers traveled to Dharamsala, where they were received as heroes by the general Tibetan population there. While the Kashag (cabinet) and the Commission of Tibetan People's Deputies were likewise pleased with the public recognition and support called forth by the demonstration, they were not, however, favorably disposed to the continued existence of the movement's leadership, the Coordinating Committee, which they saw as a potential challenge to their own authority. The official government position is presented in a statement [*gsal-bsgrags*] published in *Shes-bya* (1977), a monthly magazine put out by the Tibetan government. It is summarized and criticized in English in a letter by Samten G. Karmay (1977b). Antiestablishment sentiment ran high for some weeks in Dharamsala and elsewhere throughout the Tibetan community, but in the end the government did suceed in convincing the Coordinating Committee to disband on the grounds that, if allowed to continue, such "autonomous" leadership would further rouse that old, destructive bête noire of Tibetan history: factionalism.

The decision to dissolve the leadership of the Tibetan People's Freedom Movement did little to ameliorate tensions between the Tibetan public, who generally saw the hunger strike as a major strategic breakthrough because it was both attention getting and nonviolent, and the Dharamsala establishment, who argued that a third freedom movement (in addition to the TYC and the Movement for the Restoration of Tibet's Rightful Independence) would serve to alienate Tibetans from their government. The government's point of view convinced few nonofficial Tibetans. In fact, many people I spoke with agreed strongly with these words of a young college student: "If the leaders aren't responsive to the emotions of the people, the people will go on without their leadership."

Yet, for all the reasons discussed already, primarily the unique tradition of *chos-srid zung-'brel* ("religion and politics combined") and the supremely sacral character of the Dalai Lama's symbolic leadership, it is most unlikely that a real separatist movement could ever capture the hearts and minds of all the people. What this implies for the youth is even more disillusionment. Brought up deliberately to put their Tibetan national identity ahead of regional or sectarian considerations and schooled by the "global village" in the tactics and workings of effective international power ploys today, they can only wonder about the real meaning of the ideologies they have been taught. When they attempt to question either their own Tibetan elders or the world at large, no single answer emerges that emphasizes both realism and communal or global cooperation. With respect to both types of confrontation, then—between old- and new-style politics within the Tibetan community and between the group as a whole and the rest of the world regarding "the cause of Tibet"—the ultimate lesson is a sad one: to succeed, even only partially, one must go it alone.[7]

In addition, given the economic pressures of life in India and the individual hopes generated by being the first educated generation, this national, collective realization that Tibetans are alone in the

7. This same conclusion was told to me by one of the hunger strikers, whom I met on the third day of their fast. Moved by the calm, almost meditative resolve shown by these seven people, who appeared quite ready and willing to die for their cause, I asked what I, as a foreigner, could do to help. The answer of one of these volunteers was simple: "Thank you," she said politely, "but there's nothing you can do. We have to do it ourselves."

world has, for many young people, a personal correlative as well: "The group does indeed have a legitimate claim on my loyalties and resources, but first I must take care of my own." The self-image this fosters, however, is hardly more positive than the one that colors the hunger strikers' press release: "We Tibetans are treated as political lepers by the international community."

On two accounts, then, young Tibetans are confronted with the very real threat of alienation: as individuals vis-à-vis their group and as a stateless ethnic collectivity facing the rest of the world. It is this negative range of possibilities—of being cut off, isolated as an "other," dis-illusioned—that suggests its own positive counterbalance: regaining the "illusion"—the feeling of belonging, the sense of purposeful Tibetan selfhood—by activating the most powerful, affirmative, and sociopolitically relevant symbols of the culture. I have already shown how the word *rangzen* is being manipulated with respect to this same general goal. Now I am ready to describe its dramatized counterpart: the annual March 10 ritual of renewed commitment to "the cause of Tibet."

Tibetan Uprising Day

In the first chapter, I presented an outline of the main events of March 1959, the *illud tempus* that has become the archetype of the Tibetan people's struggle for *rangzen*, or "independence." In the two decades that have gone by since the original uprising, Tibetan communities all over the world have been rallying annually on March 10 to reenact or reaffirm key elements of that first drama. Given the very real problems of alienation, disillusionment, and confused ethnic identity that so seriously threaten young Tibetans' self-definition, this regularly recurring secular ritual does indeed act as a key scenario. Not only does it dramatize both model and means for achieving the goal of *rangzen*, but in addition it provides a way for the young generation in particular to address these problems.

This does not mean that the March 10 commemorations represent a perfected rite or that Tibetans' participation automatically guarantees them a sense of purposeful integration. In fact, the symbolization of this dramatized activity is markedly unstable, involving both familiar and alien elements, often simultaneously. My own participation as a spectator in 1977 took place in Dharamsala, where the mood of the day was decidely routinized in comparison with the ferment of protest, arrest, and jailing going on in front of the Chinese embassy in Delhi, 300 miles to the south. For me, at any rate, the most striking feature of the whole program was not the message, but the media: a mélange of symbolic attributes coming from Tibetan, Indian, and universal-modern cultural repertoires.

Like everyone else that day, I was wearing my best Tibetan clothes for the occasion. For that reason, perhaps, while walking down the mountain road to Gangchen Kyishong (the location of the Tibetan Secretariat, Library, and their official buildings) where the ceremonies would be held, I was hailed by two nuns who were burning juniper (*shug-pa*) at the side of the road. This very Tibetan symbol of auspicious benediction usually co-occurs within the context of a wider religious ritual such as the *bsangs-gsol* (incense offering) ceremony, or it may be carried out without much other ritual simply for the sake of purification. The burning of juniper I witnessed in this case—just off a road that would be traveled by hundreds of people going to the event—might thus be interpreted as an attempt by these two nuns to diffuse the religious aura as well as fragrant odor of *shug-pa*, that is, to confer benediction on the secular, political activities of the day. In any case, their comment to me as I passed acknowledged both the modern ideal of autonomous statehood as well as the very traditional Tibetan value of hospitality: "Tibetan dress suits you," said one nun by way of a greeting. "When we get our independence, come and visit us in Tibet."

The scene of the ceremony itself suggested the most famous landmark of Lhasa: the Potala. Instead of the Dalai Lama's palace, however, it was the Tibetan Library (built according to traditional Tibetan architectural style) and an enormous hanging Tibetan carpet that served as a sort of lower level backdrop for the proceedings. Officials were seated under a large canopy just in front of the library; below them (the ground drops sharply here to another level), people were gathered on a flat playing field. The key event, the Dalai Lama's personal address, was scheduled to begin at 9:00 A.M.. Arriving before that, I witnessed a truly striking clash of symbols: a Tibetan drum and bugle corps complete with drummers wearing leopard skins on their backs (I had seen similar costumes at the Indian Republic Day parade in Delhi); an imposing number of Indian (Sikh) policemen dispersed throughout the crowd; and music I recognized at once: the "Colonel Bogey March," which had no doubt been first learned in Lhasa during the time of the British mission, when the Tibetan government deliberately tried to model the Tibetan army after the British pattern. Two other important and relatively modern symbols were also incorporated into the program: the ceremony ubiquitously displayed the Tibetan flag (introduced by the Thirteenth Dalai Lama in 1912), and it began with the singing of the Tibetan national anthem (also a twentieth-century creation).

The Dalai Lama's address, which lasted barely 5 minutes, was basically a reminder of "the sufferings of the six million left in Tibet" as well as an exhortation to be faithful to primary Tibetan values such as respect and benevolence. This was followed by two reports from representatives of the executive and the legislative bodies of the Tibetan government: a member of the Kashag (cabinet) and the chairman of the Commission of Tibetan People's Deputies. All of these speeches, which were the official public highlight of the day, were over by 9:50, after which the high-ranking members of the administration accompanied the Dalai Lama into the library to view a photo exhibit documenting the progress of various Tibetan settlements located throughout India.

Outside, many of the common people then began to unfold blankets and open thermos flasks of *chang*, Tibetan barley beer, which signaled the end of the solemnity and the beginning of a picniclike atmosphere. Later in the afternoon, a sports event was held, and cultural shows put on by the Drama Society were also on the agenda. The final touch to the thoroughly routinized character of this celebration of Tibetan Uprising Day à la Dharamsala was provided by the schedule for the following week: from the twelfth to the nineteenth of March, approximately 250 officials and delegates from all over the Tibetan community in exile would assemble for the annual meeting of the entire Tibetan government.

This whole set of events—the commemoration of past martyrs, affirmations of present progress in the settlements, and commitment to ongoing bureaucracy—contrasts sharply with the fervid demonstrations taking place elsewhere on March 10, away from the headquarters of the establishment. Yet, despite the attitude of Dharamsala's critical youth, who viewed the holiday picnics, cultural shows, and general socializing as a deplorable acceptance of the status quo, the unique tone of the "capital's" March 10 ritual makes eminent sense in the light of Heusch's (1962) formulation: "the State is a challenge hurled at death" (p. 15, my translation).

For people trying to find a balance between projected hopes and remembered tragedy, it is not surprising that relative security and the institutions that seem to guarantee it would not only be recognized and affirmed but even celebrated. Furthermore, there is not the same need in Dharamsala as elsewhere for spontaneous outpourings of enthusiasm, nationalistic fervor, and strongly proclaimed ethnic self-definition. The physical presence of the Dalai Lama makes this location, like Lhasa in the past, a "holy city," which of and by itself implies charismatic leadership, regardless of how routinized all else might have become. Finally, the permanent residents of Upper Dharamsala and Gangchen Kyishong are almost exclusively Tibetan. In this situation, where the food, the clothes, the language, and the faces are only occasionally Indian, there is no sufficient foil or ethnic "other" to call forth a deliberately staged affirmation of Tibetan "self." For this reason, too, the urgent public speeches and protest marches that so characterize March 10 commemorations elsewhere in India are strongly prosaic in Dharamsala, where there is virtually no chance of demonstrators being opposed or arrested and, very significantly, no curious crowd of non-Tibetans to convince of the cause of Tibet.

Outside of Dharamsala, however, the spirit of the demonstration is decidely *not* routinized. All the attributes derived from the original drama (crowd, procession, slogans, banners, placards, national dress, flags, pictures of the Dalai Lama and his address) are displayed and employed very strategically, with great emotional involvement. (Tibetan friends and acquaintances have reported this to me many times over.) Accounts in the Tibetan press reveal another significant difference between March 10 in the capital and Uprising Day anywhere else; in more and more major world cities (Delhi, Zurich, New York, London), concerned non-Tibetans are joining the demonstrations (*Tibetan Review*, 1980c). In fact, with each passing year, the ritual appears to be more and more influenced by Tibetans' growing familiarity with public relations and media techniques.

The March 10 commemoration of Tibetan Uprising Day may thus be seen to resemble a "rite of modernization," a phrase used by Peacock (1968) in reference to *ludruk,* or Indonesian proletarian drama. According to his interpretation, such kinds of dramatization can help participants make sense of, and identify with, the process of modernization in three ways: by providing relevant and meaningful symbolic classifications; by suggesting modes of appropriate social action; and by structuring thoughts and feelings in ways that support the attendant changes (p. 6).

For the Tibetans, of course, the issue of modernization is but one part of the larger problem they face: stateless exile, with all its implications of alienation, disillusionment, and confused ethnic identity. In more generally applicable terms, then, Peacock's three points are indeed apropos. First, the symbols employed in the annual commemoration of Tibetan Uprising Day (including new, non-Tibetan symbolic forms, considerations, and media like elaborate processions to or from key local sites; the use of other languages and loudspeakers, jeeps, and other paraphernalia of public demonstrations) all help Tibetan participants to apprehend and articulate what is happening to them, not only as refugees in exile but as people attempting to keep their balance on an unstable bridge between tradition and modernity. Second, taking part in the March 10 commemoration not only increases empathy for the national cause but serves to recharge the ethnic battery, giving those who speak out in defense of Tibetan rights a renewed sense of their own and their group's worth. Third, the thoughts and feelings of the Tibetan community have, for two decades, been preoccupied with a national tragedy. Although the demonstrations commemorating Tibetan Uprising Day will never be able to obliterate the source of those bitter memories and self-recriminations, this regularly recurring ritual of politicized recommitment can at least aid in the transition from past attitudes of naive isolationism to a more realistic understanding of international realpolitik.

Chos-srid zung-'brel in New Social Contexts

In this chapter I have been presenting the experiential learning of Tibetan young adults, particularly those who have moved beyond the physical or attitudinal confines of a deliberately maintained Tibetan environment. In post–high school options and activities; ideas and ideologies; the politics of youth; and Tibetan Uprising Day one encounters example after example of conflicting demands, pressures, and even modes of life, all of which pose a real threat to this first generation's chances of achieving personal integration. Most if not all of these oppositions can be understood as involving either or both of two general types of dialectic confrontation: that between traditional and modern ways of thinking and acting and that between pure, unlived ideology and the pragmatic, compromised practices that occur as a result of actual social experience.

In both of these situations, however, it is not the case that the people concerned live in a dualistic world or that they must make either-or choices between two clearly separate realms of existence. Throughout this investigation, I have emphasized the dynamic aspects of symbolization and institutionalization; thus the emerging metaphor and scenario of this analysis draw on, as well as nourish, both traditional and modern ideals and practices. In this connection, too, I can point to significant acknowledgments of dialectic interaction that have been part and parcel of Tibetan culture for centuries: philosophical principles such as relative and absolute truth; a sophisticated system of dialectic logic; iconographic forms portraying one and the same deity as both "peaceful" and "wrathful"; a metaphysical tradition that emphasizes both active, effectual "means" and quiescent, contemplative "wisdom"; and most relevant of all from my perspective, the profoundly ambiguous figure of the Tibetan summarizing symbol, the Dalai Lama.

This sacred leader heads a government that has long been characterized by Tibetans as *chos-srid zung-'brel*, that is, one based on "religion and politics combined." Today as well, these two terms continue to be applicable to the dynamics of symbolic and social interaction; in fact, much of the material in this chapter supports just such an interpretation. As I have shown, many of the conflicts experienced in connection with post–high school activities basically involve a confrontation between untested idealism ("working for the people") and dependably expedient pragmatism (hustling or independent enterprise). A similar opposition appears even more explicitly in the ideas and ideologies encountered by these young people at this point in their lives. Because of the pure, sacred character of the supreme Tibetan authority figure, the Dalai Lama, an unequivocal policy of violent militancy, which would otherwise be regarded as most efficacious, can never be embraced unreservedly and universally as a Tibetan political strategy.

Attempts to come to terms with this impasse employ concepts and symbols clearly associated with the gestalt of *chos-srid zung-'brel*: the use of Buddhist popular tradition (Jataka stories) to justify violence; corresponding neopuritanical efforts to monitor and preserve the purity of sacred, nonviolent images; and the intellectual manipulation of the word *rangzen*, which can signify "freedom to achieve Nirvana" as well as political independence.

Extending the semantic boundaries of the words *chos*, "religion," and *srid*, "politics," to refer to "ideology" and "experience" in general, a consideration of this age group's first experiences with politics shows the same pattern: newly learned ideals of democracy, egalitarianism, and national identity contrast sharply with the old-style criteria of power still recognized and catered to by many in the Tibetan administration: region, sect, and status ascribed by birth. In addition, public demonstrations outside the Tibetan community have further confirmed this hard lesson: the noble words of communiqués and U.N. charters have little effect on the actual workings of international realpolitik.

Finally, the critical problems of potential alienation, disillusionment, and confused ethnic identity are all addressed by participation in a newly evolving secular ritual: the March 10 commemoration. Although this event may at first appear basically political, the built-in religious implications of the *rangzen* metaphor and the essential symbol of Tibetan leadership, the Dalai Lama, make the event of special significance for the experiential education of Tibetan young adults. Through it they are learning how to interpret the lessons of contemporary, alien, social experience in the familiar light of the traditionally ambiguous and therefore flexible ideology of *chos-srid zung-'brel*, "religion and politics combined."

Moreover, for the anthropologist-interpreter of all this, "the naiveté of the first certainty" likewise had to give way to questioning. Even before setting off for India I had been suitably warned by my "initiation masters" that there might be no correspondence at all between my projected research plans and my actual fieldwork situation. In this area of actual social experience, at least, I had been rather successfully innoculated against disillusionment. But in other respects, there are significant, albeit imperfect, parallels between my experience as fieldworker and the two other general problems faced by young Tibetans: potential alienation from self or group and problematic self-definition as aliens in a foreign country.

At the personal level, I can specify some of the alienating and identity-troubling consequences of doing short-term, make-it-or-break-it research in a foreign setting. Hardest for me was the disharmony I all too often felt between my experience of myself as a narrow little worker who had to fill notebooks with observations and my much less focused yet ultimately more demanding self who needed to share fears, joys, sorrows, hopes, and laughter—not to mention food and drink—with my closest Tibetan friends. My attempt to think and write more articulately about this problem took place in a 3-day marathon just before I left my fieldwork site for good. The words and ideas that took shape then I find far too revealing—about myself at least as much as about others—to incorporate in any writings intended for public readership.

In fact, my writing in general was shot through with a schizophrenia of sorts. I kept both a series of notebooks for "data" and a journal in which I detailed my reactions to the stream of impressions that began shortly after 3:00 A.M. when I stepped on the tarmac at Palam Airport, alone and dead-tired, to be instantly assailed by the strange, heavy scents and tropical air of my first New Delhi night. Had I possessed more self-knowledge at the time, I would, even in my first week in India, have recognized (and enjoyed the irony) that the journal, far more than the notebooks, would serve as the more valuable documentary support for the totality of my work.

At a more general level of reflection, a similar interpretation might be made regarding anthropologists as a group. Even before embarking on that first fieldwork venture, so many of us seem to be people who have already experienced some difficulty with self-definition relative to the perceived mainstream, be that society at large or academia in general. Witness the relatively large number of us who were attracted to anthropology as refugees from other disciplines, where we had felt dissatisfied if not alienated. Similarly, the high proportion of cross-cultural marriages and marriage attempts among us; the lives spent partially "here" and partially "there"; the wistful, almost religious reverence with which we watch, for example, films depicting the fast-disappearing lifeways of this or that group of "Gentle People" all suggest anthropologists to be inveterate non-belongers with an acute sense of nostalgia for a lost Garden of Eden.

Furthermore, the fieldwork experience as a rite of passage very definitely confirms all this socially. Following van Gennep and Turner, it is easy to identify in our disciplinary sine qua non the three stages of any transitional ritual: separation from past identity; temporary, antistructural marginality; and finally, reintegration into the community as one who has passed muster. Yet at the same time, among anthropologists, that all-important marginal stage is never quite over, even after acceptance into the post-Ph.D. "real world." Rather, we tend to embrace liminality as our more or less permanent condition, for we perceive it, even romanticized it as a generator of creative, positive ambiguity as well as a state of neither-here-nor-thereness.

So once more we are standing before the hall of mirrors, this time seeing that the reflection of an analytical concept I originally applied to the Tibetans' case now describes our own—hence the necessity of pushing further into ontological and epistemological speculation. Does the notion of liminality so aptly characterize the Tibetans' situation because it has already characterized that of my own discipline? In whose eyes? To what degree have I understood these people at all? Here the questions themselves are perhaps more revelatory than any answers I might attempt, for they point to the necessity of acknowledging this self-reflective starting point: indeterminacies as well as relevancies are an inescapable part of all hermeneutic inquiry.

Chapter Four

Reflections on Creative Sense-Making

I began this book with an imperfectly remembered quotation about the inability to grasp "truth," a theme especially relevant to philosophical and hermeneutic modes of inquiry. The quotation itself, however, did not come from Tibetan sources but from my own traditional past. Yet the book as a whole has focused, not on me, but on the attempts of young Tibetan refugees to affect and be affected by their key symbols.

This interweaving of my concerns and theirs has been quite deliberate throughout this account, for it would be extremely naive for me to try to see and interpret significant aspects of another world of meanings without at the same time acknowledging the lens effect of my own. Moreover, both they and I are further linked by the fact that we have been engaged in a similar quest. Despite the obvious differences in our situations and motivations, young Tibetans in India and I writing about what I saw there are both striving to make sense of our experience, to give it a meaningful interpretation.

Of course, the types of distanciation we must each confront are not the same. Tibetan refugees, cut off from their homeland, can no longer live and dwell within Tibetan tradition "in the naiveté of the first certainty." They must struggle to retrieve the meaning of Tibetan tradition beyond whatever loss of certitude has occurred. Their attempt, then, is to rescue the possibility of an ongoing cultural heritage by adapting and creating new meaning out of the dialectic interaction of their past and present ideologies and experience.

As for myself, I was, first of all, a foreign interpreter faced with the problem of overcoming the most obvious kind of cultural estrangement. More than that, however, I also had to confront the potentially alienating effects of such institutionalized events of the anthropological tradition as being a participant–observer, returning home from the field, writing up a dissertation, and trying to reenter the social and economic mainstream. Just as the refugees struggle to maintain an ongoing cultural heritage, the anthropologist must grapple with the problem of meaning, of making honest sense of it all. Conversely, any noncritical attempt to remain secure "in the naiveté of the first certitude" will obscure real understanding.

In the context of all of these issues, then, in this final chapter I attempt to provide some answers to the three questions I raised at the beginning. At this point, however, I can rephrase these questions in a way that should more specifically acknowledge the perspectives that have informed them. The relationship of this work to symbolic anthropology, interpretation theory, and philosophical hermeneutics can thus be expressed more explicitly in these terms:

1. How can the use and interpretation of key Tibetan symbols by Tibetan refugees in India be explained and clarified in reference to symbolic anthropology? In particular, what is the nature of the relationship between these people's situation as stateless exiles and their elaboration of the independence metaphor and the Dalai Lama symbol?
2. In general terms, how can the theoretical problem of the interpretation of textual polysemy be related to the practical situation of contextual social science investigation? More specifically, in what ways can the analogy of textual interpretation serve to inform fieldwork methodology?
3. Given the likelihood that any confrontation between the familiar and the alien will be marked by some degree of non-reflective naiveté, how can the philosophical-epistemological implications of this problem be recognized and addressed in the context of the anthropological enterprise? More precisely, what would it mean for anthropology if the concept and goal of understanding (both cross-cultural and intersubjective) were regarded as a fusion of horizons?

Ambiguity and Innovation

Throughout this book I have presented the paradigm of *chos-srid zung-'brel* ("religion and politics combined"), the symbol of the Dalai Lama, and the metaphor of independence as crucially relevant to the system of meanings evolving among Tibetan refugees today. The *rangzen* metaphor in particular impinges on contemporary events and ideologies; based on a twentieth-century neologism translatable literally as "self-power," conventionally as "independence," its extended signification has only recently begun to be consciously recognized and used by Tibetans.

This extension in usage, from conventional toward metaphoric, can be illustrated by comparing the term *rang-btsan* in the following two Tibetan sentences. The first, *bod don ni rang-btsan red* (*"Rangzen* is the 'cause' of Tibet"), expresses a meaning that Tibetans would interpret above all politically, in reference to the current Sino-Tibetan situation. In the second sentence, however— *nga rang-btsan yin* ("I'm free" [to do what I want; I'm my own boss])—the political signification of the term *rangzen* serves more as analogy than denotation, for "independence" here connotes liberation from some unspecified constraint rather than actual political domination.

Furthermore, the process of accumulating connotations works both ways. The extended meaning of the term is charged by its association with a powerfully evocative conventional understanding: "independence." In addition, the extensions of meaning suggested by the evolving metaphor add further import to the original signification. In both cases, the term *rangzen* gains in ambiguity as it becomes applied more innovatively to newer, broader referents.

This illustration, however, would hardly qualify as a full-blown example of metaphor according to the rubrics of classical rhetoric. Studies of this sort would tend to focus on the metaphoric *word* alone (e.g., "my love is a *rose*"), seeking to clarify its similarities and dissimilarities to its referent. More contemporary investigations of metaphor, however, would consider both the word and the sentence that frames it. Thus for Ricoeur and such modern semanticists as I. A. Richards, Max Black, and others (see Ricoeur, 1976: 49; also Shibles, 1972), the word does indeed serve as "the locus of the effect of metaphorical meaning." That is, it is the word *rangzen* that "shocks" hearers awake to the problematic nature of the sentence *nga rang-btsan yin* ("I'm free"), but at the same time it is the entire statement that constitutes the metaphor (Ricoeur, 1977: 66; 84).

Such an interpretation of metaphor is characteristically concerned less with resemblance and dissimilarity between word and referent than it is with the "tensive," creative potential of metaphor; thus it identifies the "place" of metaphor as "the copula of the verb *to be*" (Ricoeur, 1977: 7). This is precisely what gives so much flexible potency to Tibetan statements that equate *rangzen* with *meta*political freedom or independence: "The metaphorical 'is' at once signifies both 'is not' and 'is like'. If this is really so, we are allowed to speak of metaphorical truth, but in an equally 'tensive' sense of the word 'truth' (p. 7). In other words, the copula in such sentences sustains two opposed interpretations simultaneously. Far from threatening the meaningfulness of the total statement, however, this tensive capacity of the verb *to be* actually opens up new possibilities for interpretation. For Tibetan refugees, then, the sentence "I'm free" can indeed express a real truth.

Moreover, the extended meaning of *rangzen* affects the connotations of the original signification as well. Viewed from one perspective, that is, focusing on the word alone, the primarily political referent of the term is being nourished by a broad range of metapolitical associations: conscious and unconscious elaborations of the freedom theme (e.g., freedom to achieve Nirvana in a homeland where religion would no longer be persecuted; independent enterprise as an economic strategy for insuring cultural continuity; liberation from the constraints of certain traditional expectations). All of these attributes color the notion of *rangzen* by alluding to motifs of triumph, honor, and success (victorious warfare, dedicated spirituality, personal achievement); like the constituent morphemes of the word *rangzen* itself, this part of the metaphor fundamentally impinges on Tibetan values and stratgies pertaining to "self" and "power."

But to explain the metaphoricity of the sentence as a whole, it is not sufficient to consider only the "focus" word in isolation. Within the context of the total statement, the copula *am* or *is* both promises and cautions. In other words, the phrases "I'm free," or even "*Rangzen* is the cause of Tibet," really affirm nothing unequivocally, for the copula here also implicitly suggests "is like" and "is not exactly." Consciously, of course, the latter statement about *rangzen* hardly appears equivocal to most Tibetans at all; in fact, in one of his speeches on Tibetan Uprising Day, the Dalai Lama (1974) forthrightly proclaimed that "the cause of Tibet is the struggle of the Tibetan people to determine their own destiny." Indeed, for stateless exiles living in India, still close to Himalayan vistas, "the cause of Tibet" does primarily signify "self-determination" in the conventional political sense.

But what about those Tibetans of the diaspora who can no longer believe in political miracles? What if real independence for Tibet will never come about? Here, in fact, the equivocality of the metaphor is an asset rather than a liability. Even if the equation implied between *rangzen* and "the cause of Tibet" fails to materialize in the conventional, political sense, the broader associations of the "focus" word and the flexibility of the "frame" sentence can still serve to insure the statement's truth and viability as a metaphor, that is, tensively.

Furthermore, the *rangzen* metaphor predicates its attributes not only cognitively, as a verbal symbol, but behaviorally, through the symbolic activity or dramatic reenactment in the March 10 commemoration of Tibetan Uprising Day. Participants in this event manipulate, and are in turn affected by, powerful symbols affirming their ethnic identity: their *rang*, that is, their "self." Likewise, the principle of *btsan*, or "power," is also asserted in the course of this dramatic activity; but in this case, the primary institution to be recognized and affirmed—the Tibetan government—is fraught with an ambiguity that is not so much linguistic as actual and political. It is de facto but not de jure.

At the apex of this government-in-exile, the figure of the Dalai Lama is marked by even greater ambiguity: he is both spiritual, transcendent incarnation and temporal, immanent leader. Furthermore, he is the symbolic head of an institution that has traditionally been associated with a paradigm (religion and politics combined) that explicitly acknowledges power in both its dangerous and benevolent aspects, with the potential for violence and compassion mutually counterpoised. In view of all this, then, how can Tibetans' interpretation of this miraculous yet also routinized symbol be explained and clarified in more general, theoretical terms?

As I have shown, the figure and institution of the Dalai Lama serves to sum up and express for Tibetans the meaning of "Tibetanness" in a powerfully affective way. In this particular sociocultural context especially, this symbol's capacity to inspire commitment, to draw together people, beliefs, meanings, and strategies, is indeed rooted in Tibetans' existential situation: first in their prior history and tradition, now in their experience as stateless refugees. In this connection, Ricoeur's (1976) observation is apt indeed, given further qualification: "This bound character of symbols makes all the difference between a symbol and a metaphor. The latter is a free invention of discourse; the former is bound to the cosmos"(p. 61).

Such a distinction between symbol-cosmos and metaphor-discourse is, of course, an ideal one, and it is this fact that enables Ricoeur (1976) to develop his discussion so lucidly. Accordingly, he views metaphor as linguistic procedure, that is, as a form of predication that can clarify by making apprehension explicitly semantic. Correspondingly, symbols for him have an essentially presemantic aspect, reaching down to the nonexplicit depths of human experience (p. 69). But as in the case of the *rangzen* metaphor and the symbol of the Dalai Lama, neither image exists in pure form. Not only does the metaphor clarify by linguistic predication, but, very much rooted in specific human experience, it animates sociopolitical activity and drama too. Similarly, not only is the figure and institution of the Dalai Lama "bound to the cosmos," but in addition, it is and has been dependent on the verbal elaboration of Tibetan discourse for five centuries.

In both cases, then, the freedom and boundedness of these key cultural images is relative, ultimately conditioned by the particular existential situation of the human beings who have created and elaborated them. It is this point, in fact, that brings the discussion back to the question posed at the beginning: What is the nature of the relationship between Tibetan refugees' existence as stateless exiles and their interpretation and elaboration of the independence metaphor and the Dalai Lama symbol?

Stated briefly, the characteristic that appears to predominate both in the Tibetan refugees' sociopolitical situation and in their contemporary key symbols is this: creative ambiguity. Living as they are in a liminal state of noncitizenship, these people, struggling to endure as a collectivity, are vitally involved in apprehending and articulating the dialectical tensions that threaten yet also in some measure invigorate them. But dialectical confrontation, the interaction of thesis and antithesis, does not create its synthesis ex nihilo. Rather, the impelling forces of tradition and modernity; violence and nonviolence; perpetuity and change; ideology and experience—all of these and other relevant oppositions—generate forms that may be new but that are still informed by antecedent ideas and behavior patterns.

Furthermore, this generation of new symbolic forms is especially influential for, and influenced by, the "real" new generation: the youth. Brought up in a society within a society, where power and legitimacy are ambiguous and where self-identity is particularly difficult to achieve, these children and young adults are being doubly socialized: both through institutions planned to be as traditional as possible, and through new, sometimes radically different social experience. For them, specifically the young Tibetan refugees in India, the most crucial problem, that of self and group definition, is also the fundamental issue underlying the newly emerging metaphor of *rangzen*. Such a coincidence is not accidental, for as Turner (1974) points out, "Root paradigms emerge in life crises, whether of groups or individuals, whether institutionalized or compelled by unforseen events" (p. 64). Even more to the point, "paradigms of this fundamental sort reach down to irreducible life stances of individuals, passing beneath conscious prehension to a fiduciary hold on what they sense to be axiomatic values, matters literally of life or death"(p. 64).

For Tibetan culture to survive, even in adapted form, Tibetan people must continue to define themselves as such. For this to occur, mere cultural preservation is not sufficient; innovation, too, must continue to enliven the cultural repertoire. In their quest for meaningful self- and group identity, Tibetan refugees are indeed engaging in this very process, especially as they manipulate and are affected by the tensive ambiguity that so characterizes their situation.

Polysemy and Interpretation

I have up to now been considering specific instances of ambiguity within a particular ethnographic setting. The general issue of ambiguity can also be explored from another perspective: that of interpretation theory. Seen in this light, the problem of polysemy and its interpretation is relevant not only in the case of linguistic texts but sociocultural contexts as well. Accordingly, insights directly applicable to textual interpretation can, by analogy, serve to clarify corresponding aspects of fieldwork methodology with this proviso in mind: the term *text* here is to be understood not merely as "static, written, objective form" but also and even primarily as intersubjective "discourse," "*parole*," or "speech event."

It is hardly a novel idea, of course, that hermeneutic theory may be profitably employed as part of social science methodology. Despite this, however, anthropologists have tended to overlook the more personal implications of this text-context analogy, especially in reference to one aspect of the anthropological enterprise: their own reflexive participation in it. Such implications—the oversight as well as its correction—can ultimately be linked with the notion of *understanding* (both cross-cultural and intersubjective) considered, in the sense of philosophical hermeneutics, as "a fusion of horizons." Before proceeding to examine this final point, however, I should clarify both types of investigations—interpreting polysemy in texts and discourses and interpreting ambiguity in sociocultural situations—with respect to the object, techniques, and implications of each.

Any attempt at delimiting the object of a particular kind of research must begin by acknowledging the issue of ontologies and epistemologies. Accordingly, researchers in any line of study must confront the following two questions: What is the nature of the reality or realities to be examined? In this particular mode of investigation, what are the criteria that determine if the "findings" or "knowledge" thus gained are valid? Obviously, theologians and engineers would elaborate very different responses in each case. So, too, should anthropologists.

On the other hand, those anthropologists who specialize in the study of symbolic systems (language, religion, and aesthetics would be the ideal types here, but any nonbiological system could be so considered) are in fact quite close to literary or linguistic analysts in this respect at least: the object of their study involves a particular kind of encoding or disclosure. It is here, in reference to this methodological clarification of objectives, that hermeneutic theory can be beneficially suggestive. It can shed light on the ontological and epistemological implications of the attempt to rescue meaning.

Thus the question How can I really know what this text or that person means? is in fact inappropriate here, for valid knowledge in this type of investigation is not defined in terms of the investigator apprehending the author's or actor's subjective intention. Rather, the nature of the realities in question (e.g., the words, forms, gestures, or acts being interpreted as symbols) demands that more dialectic, open criteria be used to determine the validity of the interpretation. Instead of asking What has the author or actor intended by this? the more relevant question would thus be What is this discourse or action *about*?

Seen in this light, polysemy is not pathology, as the ordinary language philosophers have already pointed out. In fact, it is precisely because of its potential for multivocality that ordinary language (as distinct from the ideal language of mathematics and logic) can and does serve as the basis for symbolic discourse. Concomitantly, the interpretation of nonlinguistic symbols too can be more adequately described—to use Ricoeur's terms (1971)—as an attempt to "disclose" or "open up an ontological world." In other words, whenever the object of social science research involves the attempt to interpret ambiguity, to understanding the meaning of symbolic words, forms, or (inter)actions, what is really put into play is a vital, ongoing, and dialectic connection between two discourses: the world of the person(s) being investigated, and the world of the person(s) doing the investigation. "Understanding" in this sense, then, would involve transcending one's immediate situation by allowing all the possible referents and relevancies of either discourse to enlarge one's ontological world.

As far as the technique of this process is concerned, once again the anthropological enterprise can be clarified by considering the approached used in the interpretation of written texts. In this connection, hermeneutic theory has been especially concerned with a situation that indeed parallels cross-cultural research: how can understanding take place in cases where the symbolic documents being studied are the products of another era, society, or world view?

The answer proposed by hermeneutic theory involves the notion of "the hermeneutic circle," a dialectic, back-and-forth movement between "belief" (characterized as a willingness to listen, to grant that the text or symbol or subject of interpretation has something "true" to say) and an "understanding" that must necessarily entail critical reflection (Ihde, 1971: 141, 162). For the anthropologist especially, such a willingness to listen with all sensual and imaginative faculties wide open would seem absolutely essential. But it is important to note that this kind of openness is not naive; that is, it neither courts nor sustains illusion. "Suspicion," too is called for by hermeneutic theory, not only in reference to strange "other" phenomena but also in respect to one's own presuppositions about them.

Ricoeur (1971, 1976, 1981) develops these ideas even further in connection with his discussion of the relationship between understanding and explanation in the social sciences, a problem that has occupied theorists since Wilhelm Dilthey. By insisting on the fact that "meaningfully oriented behavior" has both subjective and objective aspects, he is able to justify both "the genius of guessing" and "the scientific character of validation" in relation to the research endeavor here. In other words, ethnographic data can indeed be right or wrong. Yet, any judgment about an ultimately superior, absolutely comprehensive interpretation is truly impossible; it can never be more than a guess.

To refer this discussion back to my Tibetan study, it is certainly the case that the data I acquired and have been presenting could have been more complete; that I could have missed or misunderstood significant information; that the presuppositions that preceded my hundreds of encounters with Tibetans could have been based on ignorant mistakes. The awareness of such possibilities occurring in the fieldwork enterprise has sent shudders down the spines of countless ethnographers; it is quite beside the point to talk of "relatively better or worse interpretations" in connection with the attempt to *explain* objectifiable facts.

But my attempts to *interpret* the ambiguous figure of the Dalai Lama and to guess at the reasons why *rangzen* means so much to Tibetans can only be challenged by more likely interpretations. This is not a result of my inability (or other anthropologists' superior ability) to "get into the heads" of the people I investigated or of the Tibetans' inability to communicate the "real meaning" of it all. Rather, such powerfully evocative, multivalent key symbols are just that: polysemic. My attempt to understand these images in this sociocultural context must, then, acknowledge these two facts: multiple meanings are simultaneously relevant and realizable here, and the process of trying to interpret such polysemy, especially in reference to an ontological world alien to me, impinges directly on my own ontological world.

These two points are particularly significant in respect to the final topic of this concluding chapter: the reflexive implications of an-thropologizing. Before proceeding to these last considerations, how-ever, the issue of polysemy and its interpretation should be clarified from one more angle: the factor of personal involvement or detach-ment in this kind of research endeavor.

Once again, modern (post-Romanticist) hermeneutic theory offers a conceptualization that is both suggestive and relevant vis-à-vis the anthropological enterprise: the dialectic of distanciation and appro-priation. To quote Ricoeur (1976):

> To appropriate is to make "one's own" what was "alien." Be-cause there is a general need for making our own what is for-eign to us, there is a general problem of distanciation. Dis-tance, then, is not simply a fact, a given, just the actual spatial and temporal gap between us and the appearance of such and such work of art or discourse. It is a dialectical trait, the princi-ple of a struggle between the otherness that transforms all spa-tial and temporal distance into cultural estrangement and the ownness by which all understanding aims at the extension of self-understanding. Distanciation is not a qualitative phenome-non; it is the dynamic counterpart of our need, our interest, and our effort to overcome cultural estrangement. (p. 43)

These ideas about interpreting "foreign" texts can be applied with little qualification to the situation of engaging in anthropological fieldwork. Moreover, another statement by Ricoeur (1977) can like-wise serve to describe the fieldwork endeavor by analogy: "To under-stand discourse is to interpret the actualizations of its polysemic val-ues according to the persmissions and suggestions proposed by the context" (p. 322).

To some degree, the human, personal implications of trying to make one's own what is alien, of being sensitive to the "permissions and suggestions" proposed by, in this case, the fieldwork experience, have already been noted by numerous anthropologists, particularly

by those who have consciously and deliberately included themselves in their ethnographies. Nonetheless, such writing has not always been sufficiently explicit about the relationship of these issues
to the problem of self-knowledge. While words and phrases like "involvement" and "detachment" and "stepping in and out of society"
(Powdermaker, 1966) certainly do describe the subjective–objective
demands of participant observation methodology, the reflexive implications of the endeavor to overcome cultural estrangement have
not always been fully acknowledged.

Despite the great emphasis given by anthropology to the principle
of cultural relativity (at least in reference to cross-cultural standards
of "goodness" and "beauty," if not necessarily "truth"), the critical
roots of this prejudice against prejudice have rarely, until recently, in
our discipline been an object for reflection. Moreover, our general
failure to acknowledge consciously the implications of our own tradition, that is, our generally naive acceptance of Enlightenment assumptions and prejudgments about the nature of truth, certainly intrudes in the way of overcoming cultural estrangement. In sum, if
we are to be at all self-aware about what it means to interpret polysemy according to the permissions and suggestions proposed by "the
others," that is, by the people we study, we must begin by recognizing that we, too, proceed in our quest for meaning from a predefined
ontological world whose horizon is limited.

Understanding as Fusion of Horizons

All of the preceding issues and considerations can
now serve as background for the final question posed at the beginning of this chapter: Given the likelihood that any confrontation
between the familiar and the alien will be marked by some degree
of nonreflective naiveté, how can the philosophical and epistemological implications of this problem be recognized and addressed in
the context of the anthropological enterprise? More precisely, what
would it mean for anthropology if the concept and goal of understanding, both cross-cultural and intersubjective, were regarded as a
fusion of horizons?

This latter concept, elaborated most thoroughly by the modern hermeneutic philosopher Gadamer, is fundamentally critical in its focus on historicity, or tradition in relation to understanding. Restating this in Gadamer's (1975/1960) own words:

> The horizon is the range of vision that includes everything that can be seen from a particular vantage point. . . . The word has been used in philosophy since Nietzsche and Husserl to characterize the way in which thought is tied to its finite determination, and the nature of the law of the expansion of the range of vision (p. 269)

Furthermore, "every experience has implicit horizons of before and after, and finally merges with the continuum of the experience present in the before and after to form one flow of experience" (p. 216). Finally, Gadamer explicitly defines *fusion of horizons* in these terms: "It is part of real understanding . . . that we regain the concepts of our own comprehension of them" (p. 337).

The implications of these ideas for anthropology, particularly in respect to the fieldwork experience, are extremely significant. First, this kind of conceptualization of *understanding* challenges anthropologists to formulate a critical (as opposed to naive) working definition of *openness* vis-à-vis other cultures' ontological worlds. In other words, by recognizing the implicit horizons of "before and after" (or "their tradition" and "ours") in every encounter with native informants, anthropologists engaged in collecting data would at the same time acknowledge that their discourse, too, proceeds from a finite range of vision. In addition, the central problem of this entire book, that of rescuing meaning, can now, with the above ideas in mind, be considered beyond the particular situation of the Tibetan diaspora. In fact, this problem concerns everyone; it is the quest for meaning beyond "the naiveté of the first certainty."

To begin with the first issue, the kind of openness that Gadamer (1975/1960) has in mind is fundamentally philosophical in nature; it has the structure of a question rooted in "the knowledge of not knowing" (p. 325). At first glance, this might also seem to characterize the anthropologist who sincerely asks questions about this or that ritual, kinship connection, or trading pattern, all the while being open to strange answers, beliefs, behaviors, and even (and especially!) dietary preferences. But in fact, the openness of philosophical hermeneutics has little to do with willingness to eat roased caterpillars; furthermore, it definitely does not require or even recommend trying to forget or deny the answers, beliefs, and practices of one's own culture in order to understand those of another.

Rather, the notion of openness that Gadamer (1975/1960) espouses is one that recognizes and even affirms, with qualifications, "prejudice" in its etymological, pre-Englightenment sense: "prejudice" as "prejudgments." What distinguishes this from mere arrogant ethnocentricism is the reflexive quality it entails. To paraphrase Gadamer (who is in fact writing here about the interpretation of written texts), every encounter with another tradition or culture involves the experience of the tension between that tradition and our own. The task of cross-cultural intrepretation consists in not covering up this tension by attempting a naive assimilation. Stated positively, this task would consciously seek to bring this tension out into the open (p. 273).

But the goal here is not merely to confront the other or ourselves with an affirmation of the distance or tension that separates us. More than this, such a recognition should also acknowledge the questionableness of our own tradition as well. In fact, for Gadamer (1975/1960), it is this notion of questioning (much more than answering) that is crucially related to the ideal of understanding; for questioning is not the positing, but the testing, of possibilities (p. 338). That is, questioning brings out into the open both the indeterminacies of and the relevant alternatives to what is being questioned (pp. 326–327). Accordingly, understanding takes place not when we have the answer but when we understand the question to which the answer may apply (p. 337). Thus "questioning" in this sense is both reconstructive and reflexive. It seeks to identify the range of vision that has informed the other tradition's questions and answers, and it also refers back to the horizon of our own tradition, trying to acknowledge there the prejudgments that make it possible for us even to attempt understanding.

Given the idea that understanding the other has more to do with comprehending the other's implicit questions than with explicit answers, one may look with fresh insight at this aspect of the fieldwork experience: obtaining native explanations that are at variance with our own culture's ontological and epistemological presuppositions. Thus Tibetan statements based on the belief in reincarnation or the principle of karma should prompt us to acknowledge here not only their horizons but ours as well. The focus in this type of investigation would not be limited to the question What do they mean by "reincarnation" or "karma"? It would also ask the question What questions in Tibetan tradition are being addressed by these particular answers? (see Epstein, 1977). Moreover, a reflexive consideration would also be in order here: What questions in our own tradition make us so quick to say "of course" or "of course not" in reference to these Tibetan ideas about continuity and causation?

By employing in this critical way such concepts as *openness*, *questioning*, and *understanding*, anthropologists can indeed attempt to make estrangement and distanciation productive, as the hermeneuticians would say. Moreover, this kind of cross-cultural research would also have the potential to address and challenge a weakness in our general intellectual tradition: the uncritical assumption that, after all is said and done in the name of cultural relativity, it is still *our* ontological world and *our* epistemological criteria that have primary access to "real" truth.

Attempts to rescue meaning, then, can and do acknowledge all sorts of estrangements. In cases where the gap or distanciation separates two different cultures, interpretation can best proceed when both sets of presuppositions, theirs and ours, are first recognized, then reflected upon. In other cases, that is, in situations where meaning has been lost or threatened within a particular culture, the familiar/alien dialectic will also be strongly marked by considerations of past/present.

With respect to the specific situation I present in this book, all of these points do indeed seem applicable. Young Tibetan refugees in India are engaging in innovative attempts to rescue meaning. They are interpreting and reinterpreting two key Tibetan symbols, the image of the Dalai Lama and the motif of independence, seeking in this way to forge viable links between tradition and modernity, perpetuity and change, ideology and experience. The major problems that confront them here all involve potential negation of these links. They include the threat of alienation from self or other Tibetans; disillusionment over hopes and expectations that will likely never come true; and confused ethnic identity in the wake of the Tibetan diaspora.

In the light of my discussion of *understanding* as a "fusion of horizons," it is instructive to recall the basis for Tibetans' attempted

solutions to these problems: a reaffirmation, at a new level of awareness, of the past and familiar Tibetan gestalt of *chos-srid zung-'brel*
("religion and politics combined"). In this connection, Gadamer's
(1975/1960) words are apt indeed: "A horizon is not a rigid frontier,
but something that moves with one and invites one to advance further" (p. 217).

This same invitation to use one's past or present range of vision in
order to advance further extends to us, the interpreters, too. By considering the concept and the goal of cross-cultural understanding as
a fusion of horizons, that is, as a critical, self-reflective encounter
between "their" range of vision and "ours," the gain for anthropology
would not merely be better ethnographies. More than that, such an
attempt at reflexive understanding would fundamentally and creatively increase our own self-knowledge as well.

Appendix

Continuity and Change in the Tibetan Electoral System

From 1960 to the present, the legislative branch of the Tibetan government-in-exile has undergone several significant changes in its electoral system. At the same time, however, the key symbol of the Dalai Lama has lost none of its power to stand above special interest groups' mundane jostlings for political authority.

When elections were first held, in 1960, for the Commission of Tibetan People's Deputies, 13 people were selected for these positions: 3 lay members from each of the three recognized regions of Tibet (Dbus-Gtsang, Amdo, and Khams), and 1 member from each of the four main Tibetan Buddhist sects. In 1963 the total number of representatives was raised to 17; the Dalai Lama nominated one member, and three positions (one for each region) were to be reserved for women. The latter policy was subsequently rescinded during International Women's Year (1975) on the grounds that a preferential quota system, which in effect denied the possibility of equal competition, was actually discriminatory to women.

In 1977 a further change was made in the composition of the commission (called the assembly as of 1980). At the request of the Tibetan Bonpo community, the Dalai Lama gave his consent for a Bonpo representative to be included as well. This move is significant: Bonpos—or "followers of Bon," a native Tibetan religion often and incorrectly considered the direct survival of an ancient, pre-Buddhist shamanistic cult—are for that reason often regarded as marginal by orthodox Tibetan Buddhists. While it is true that the Bonpos worship Ston-pa Gshen-rab instead of the Sakyamuni Buddha, their liturgy, monastic life, iconographic forms, and scriptures are virtually indistinguishable from the corresponding Buddhist forms, which they obviously absorbed and adapted over the course of centuries of parallel existence in Tibet. (The Norwegian researcher Kvaerne (1976a, 1976b), who has worked in a Bonpo community in Himachal Pradesh near Simla, has written two articles dealing with Buddhist-Bonpo similarities and differences.)

Following the news of the policy change in favor of Bonpo representation, the former president of the Tibetan Youth Congress, which had unsuccessfully tried to achieve the same goal through the "proper" channels, wrote a letter to the editor in which he congratulated the Bonpo community for "having the courage to make a direct appeal to His Holiness the Dalai Lama in order to obtain their legitimate rights in spite of repeated refusal by the concerned authorities" (Lodi Gyaltsen Gyari 1977).

In 1978 the TYC attempted to make two more changes in the electoral system. To eliminate what they perceived as its regional and sectarian basis, they first tried to transfer the five sectarian (i.e., religious) deputies to the Council of Religious and Cultural Affairs and, second, to give every Tibetan the right to vote for a representative from any of the three Tibetan regions instead of being limited to voting for a representative of his "home" area. The National Working Committee of the Tibetan government turned down the proposal for the stated reason that, were these changes to occur, "the Tibetans in Tibet might look upon the Commission [of People's Deputies] as 'unrepresentative'" (*Tibetan Review*, 1978b; see also *Tibetan Review*, 1978d, 1978e).

Despite the committee's rejection of the TYC's proposal as suggested, the concern about regionalism was officially addressed in 1982 by another set of changes in election procedures. First, the number of regional (lay) deputies was reduced from 12 to 6 (2 per region instead of the former 4). Moreover, the 1982 elections marked the beginning of the new policy by which Tibetans select candidates (6 in all) from all three regions instead of voting for 4 representatives only from their "home" regions. The number of religious deputies has remained the same.

Finally, in response to the fears and protests of Tibetans originally from Khams and Amdo concerning the numerical predominance of Tibetans originally from central Tibet, another change has been made. As explained in the August 1982 issue of *Tibetan Review* (1982c), "in order to stop the controversy" surrounding the Tibetan election system, the Dalai Lama himself now selects the final six deputies from a list of candidates previously nominated in local elections. Commenting on the consequences of this last change, a *Tibetan Review* editorial (1982a) states that, "unlike any other changes made previously, this one has not prompted any controversy or overt resentment. More importantly, this is the first time that none of the deputies from the last Assembly has been reinstated" (p. 3). Clearly, the sacred symbol of the Dalai Lama has once again been used to nullify the dangerously divisive effects of secular contestations for power.

References

Andrugtsang, Gompo Tashi
1973   Four Rivers, Six Ranges: Reminiscences of the Resistance
                Movement in Tibet. Dharamsala: Information and
                Publicity Office of H. H. the Dalai Lama.

Bacot, J.; F. W. Thomas; and C. Toussaint
1940–1946   Documents de Touen-houang relatifs à l'histoire du Tibet.
                Paris Annales du Musée Guimet. Bibliothèque d'études,
                vol. 51.

Balandier, Georges
1972   Political Anthropology. Trans. by A. M. Sheridan Smith.
                Harmondsworth: Penguin. (French original 1967)

Barth, Fredrik
1969   Ethnic Groups and Boundaries: The Social Organization of
                Cultural Differences. Boston: Little, Brown.

Bharati, Agehananda
1969   The Tantric Tradition. 2d ed. London: Rider.

Boon, James A.
1972   From Symbolism to Structuralism: Lévi-Strauss in a
                Literary Tradition. New York: Harper & Row.

Burke, Kenneth
1966   Language as Symbolic Action. Berkeley and Los Angeles:
                University of California Press.

Cohen, Abner
1976   Two-dimensional Man: An Essay on the Anthropology
                of Power and Symbolism in Complex Society. Reprint.
                Berkeley and Los Angeles: University of California Press.

Constitution of Tibet
1963   New Delhi: Bureau of H. H. the Dalai Lama.

Corlin, Claes
1975   "The Nation in Your Mind: Continuity and Change among
                Tibetan Refugees in Nepal." Ph.D. dissertation, University
                of Gothenburg.

Dalai Lama XIV
1962   My Land and My People. New York: McGraw-Hill.

1969   "India and Tibet." Address given to the Servants of the
              People Society, August 4, 1966. Reprinted in Tibetan
              Review, January-February, pp. 12–14.
1974   "What Is Tibet's Cause?" March 10 address reprinted in
              Tibetan Review, March, p. 6.

Das, Sarat Chandra
1970   A Tibetan-English Dictionary. 2d ed. Delhi: Motilal
              Banarsidass.

Dawa Dhondup
1976   "Distribution of Scholarships." Tibetan Review, October,
              pp. 32–33.

Dawa Norbu
1973   "What Tibet Did in 2100 Years." Tibetan Review, March,
              pp. 8–9.
1974   Red Star over Tibet. London: Collins.

Denwood, Philip
1975   "Independent Mongolia and Autonomous Tibet." Tibetan
              Review, February–March, pp. 12–17.

De Vos, George
1975   "Ethnic Pluralism: Conflict and Accommodation."
              Pp. 5–41 in Ethnic Identity: Cultural Continuities and
              Change, edited by George De Vos and Lola Romanucci-
              Ross. Palo Alto: Mayfield.

De Vos, George, and Lola Romanucci-Ross
1975   "Ethnicity: Vessel of Meaning and Emblem of Contrast."
              Pp. 363–390 in Ethnic Identity. See De Vos, 1975.

Dhondup, K.
1977a   Letter. Tibetan Review, July, p. 34.
1977b   Letter. Tibetan Review, November, pp. 29–30.

Dhondup Choedon
1978   Life in the Red Flag People's Commune. Dharamsala:
              Information Office of H. H. the Dalai Lama.

Dumont, Jean-Paul
1978   The Headman and I: Ambiguity and Ambivalence in the
              Fieldwork Experience. Austin: University of Texas Press.

Epstein, Lawrence
1977   "Causation in Tibetan Religion: Duality and Its
              Transformations." Ph.D. dissertation, University of
              Washington, Seattle.

Fernandez, James
1974   "The Mission of Metaphor in Expressive Culture. Current
               Anthropology, 15(2): 119–145.
1977   "The Performance of Ritual Metaphors." Pp. 100–131 in
               The Social Use of Metaphor. *See* Sapir and Crocker, 1975.

Fortes, Meyer
1970   "Social and Psychological Aspects of Education in
               Taleland." Pp. 54–91 in From Child to Adult. *See*
               Middleton, 1970.

Fraser, John
1981   "The National Minorities of China." Tibetan Review, June,
               pp. 17–23. Reprinted from Fraser's The Chinese: Portrait of
               a People. New York: Summit, 1980.

Gadamer, Hans-Georg
1975   Truth and Method. New York: Continuum Publishing.
               (German original 1960)
1976   Philosophical Hermeneutics. Trans. and edited by David
               Linge. Berkeley and Los Angeles: University of California
               Press.

Geertz, Clifford
1972   "Deep Play: Notes on the Balinese Cockfight." Daedalus,
               101: 1–37.
Gennep, Arnold van
1960   The Rites of Passage. Trans. Monika B. Vizedom and
               Gabrielle L. Caffee. Chicago: University of Chicago Press.
               (French original 1908)

Goldstein, Chunden Surkhang
n.d.   "Secular Education in Lhasa." Unpublished manuscript,
               University of Washington, Inner Asia Seminar, Seattle.

Goldstein, Melvyn
1968   "An Anthropological Study of the Tibetan Political
               System." Ph.D. dissertation, University of Washington,
               Seattle.
1973   "The Circulation of Estates in Tibet: Reincarnation, Land
               and Politics." Journal of Asian Studies, 3:444–455.
1975a   Tibetan-English Dictionary of Modern Tibetan.
               Kathmandu. Ratna Pustak Bhandar.
1975b   "Tibetan Refugees in South India: A New Face to the Indo-
               Tibetan Inferface." Tibet Society Bulletin, 9:12–29.

Grunfeld, A. Tom
1981   "Tibetan History: A Somewhat Different Approach.
                    "Tibetan Review, June, pp. 8–14.

Gupta, D. K.
1973   "Dalai Lama's Dual Tactics." Tibetan Review,
                    October–November, pp. 16–17.

Haarh, Erik
1969   The Yarlung Dynasty. Copenhagen: Gad's Forlag.

Heusch, Luc de
1962   "Pour une dialectic de la sacralité du pouvoir." Pp. 15–47
                    in Le Pouvoir et la Sacre. Brussels: Annales du Centre
                    d'étude des religions.

Hoffman, Helmut
1961   The Religions of Tibet. Trans. by Edward Fitzgerald.
                    London: Allen & Unwin. (German original 1956).

Hopkins, Jeffrey
1973   "Emptiness Is Dynamic and Rich." Tibetan Review,
                    October–November, pp. 23–26.

Ihde, Don
1971   Hermeneutic Phenomenology: The Philosophy of Paul
                    Ricoeur. Evanston, Ill.: Northwestern University Press.

Kaminski, Ignacy-Marek
1980   The State of Ambiguity: Studies of Gypsy Refugees.
                    Gothenburg: University of Gothenburg.

Karan, Pradyumna Prasad
1976   The Changing Face of Tibet: The Impact of Chinese
                    Communist Ideology on the Landscape. Lexington:
                    University Press of Kentucky.

Keller, Stephen
1975   Uprooting and Social Change: The Role of Refugees in
                    Development. Delhi: Manohar.

Khan, T. A.
1976   "Stone Building Is No School." Tibetan Review, June–July,
                    pp. 20–21.

Kvaerne, Per
1976a   "The Genesis of the Tibetan Buddhist Tradition." Tibetan
                    Review, March, pp. 9–15.
1976b   "Who Are the Bonpos?" Tibetan Review, September,
                    pp. 30–33.

Lhakpa Tsering
1976   "You Speak Too Loud." Tibetan Review, October, p. 32.

Linge, David
1976   "Editor's Introduction." Pp. xi–lvii in Philosophical
                       Hermeneutics. *See* Gadamer, 1976.

Lodi Gyaltsen Gyari
1976   "The Dynamics of a Silent Struggle." Rangzen, Autumn,
                       pp. 5–8.

March:
1976   A Bimonthly Information Bulletin of the Delhi Tibetan
                       Youth Congress 3(2).

Marcus, George E., and Dick Cushman
1982   "Ethnographies as Texts." Pp. 25–69 in Annual Review of
                       Anthropology, edited by Bernard Siegel. Stanford: Stanford
                       University Press.

Mayer, Philip
1970   "Introduction." Pp. xiii–xxx in Socialization: The
                       Approach from Social Anthropology. London: Tavistock.

Mehra, Parshotam Lal
1968   The Younghusband Expedition. New York: Asia Publishing
                       House.

Messerschmidt, Donald
1976   "Innovation in Adaptation: Tibetan Immigrants in the
                       United States." Tibet Society Bulletin, 10:48–70.

Middleton, John, ed.
1970   "Preface." Pp. xi–xx in From Child to Adult: Studies in the
                       Anthropology of Education. Austin: University of Texas
                       Press.

Murphy, Henry B. M.
1955   Flight and Resettlement. Paris: UNESCO.

New Dawn Second Grade Textbook ('dzin-gra gnyis-pa'i slob-deb skya-rengs
gsar-pa)
1964   Dharamsala: Tibetan Cultural Printing Press.

Nowak, Margaret
1978a   "The Education of Young Tibetans in India: Cultural
                       Preservation or Agent for Change?" Pp. 191–198 in
                       Tibetan Studies, edited by Martin Brauen and Per Kvaerne.
                       Zurich: Völkerkundemuseum der Universität Zürich.
1978b   "Liminal 'Self,' Ambiguous 'Power': The Genesis of the

'Rangzen' Metaphor among Tibetan Youth in India." Ph.D. dissertation, University of Washington, Seattle.

1980   "Change and Differentiation in Tibetan Sex Roles: The New Adult Generation in India." Pp. 219–225 in Tibetan Studies in Honour of Hugh Richardson, edited by Michael Aris and Aung San Suu Kyi. Proceedings of the International Seminar on Tibetan Studies, Oxford, 1979. Warminster: Aris & Phillips.

Ortner, Sherry B.
1973   "On Key Symbols." American Anthropologist, 75:1338–1346.

Ott-Marti, Anna Elizabeth
1971   Tibeter in der Schweiz: Kulturelle Verhaltensweisen im Wandel. Erlenbach-Zurich: Eugen Rentsch.
1976   "Problems of Tibetan Integration in Switzerland." Ethnologia Europea, 9 (1):43–52.

Pasang Dhondup
1977   "Appeals from People." Tibetan Review, June 1977: 26.

Peacock, James L.
1968   Rites of Modernization: Symbolic and Social Aspects of Indonesian Proletarian Drama. Chicago: University of Chicago Press.

Petech, Luciano
1939   A Study on the Chronicles of Ladakh. Calcutta: n.p.
1950   China and Tibet in the Early Eighteenth Century: History of the Establishment of the Chinese Protectorate in Tibet. Leiden: Brill.

Phurbu Tsering
1976   "Profiles: A Skilled Actor and a Remarkable Opera Star." Rangzen, Summer, pp. 20–24.

Pott, Peter H.
1968   The Art of Tibet. Pp. 153–236 in The Art of Burma, Korea and Tibet by Alexander B. Griswold, Chewon Kim, and Peter H. Pott. New York: Greystone.

Powdermaker, Hortense
1966   Stranger and Friend: The Way of an Anthropologist. New York: Norton.

Quillen, I. James
1955   "A Conception of Education." Pp. 23–26 in Education and Anthropology. Stanford, Calif.: Stanford University Press.

Rabinow, Paul
1977   Reflections on Fieldwork in Morocco. Berkeley and Los
              Angeles: University of California Press.

Rangzen
197⎵a   "We Shall Not Cease from Exploration. . ." Summer,
              pp. 2–8.
1976b   "A Yak in Madison Avenue." Summer, pp. 12–20.
1977   "The Fourth Working Committee Meeting and the
              Meaning of Freedom." Spring, pp. 1–3.

Read, Kenneth E.
1980   Other Voices: The Style of a Male Homosexual Tavern.
              Novato, Calif.: Chandler & Sharp.

Richardson, Hugh E.
1962   A Short History of Tibet. New York: Dutton. (Published in
              England as Tibet and Its History)

Ricoeur, Paul
1963   "Structure et herméneutic." Esprit 322:596–627.
1967   "La structure, le mot, l'événement." Esprit 360:801–821.
1971   "The Model of the Text: Meaningful Action Considered
              as Text." Social Research, 38:529–562.
1976   Interpretation Theory: Discourse and the Surplus of
              Meaning. Fort Worth: Texas Christian University Press.
1977   The Rule of Metaphor: Multi-disciplinary Studies in the
              Creation of Meaning in Language. Toronto: Uhiversity of
              Toronto Press.
1981   Hermeneutics and the Human Science: Essays on
              Language, Action and Interpretation. Cambridge:
              Cambridge University Press.

Roerich, George N., trans.
1976   The Blue Annals. Delhi: Motilal Banarsidass.

Samdong Rinpoche
1977   "The Social and Political Strata in Buddhist Thought."
              Tibet Journal, 2(1):1–9.

Samten G. Karmay
1977a   "Religion: A Major Cause of Tibetan Disunity." Tibetan
              Review, May, pp. 25–26.
1977b   Letter. Tibetan Review, June, pp. 24–25.

Sapir, J. David, and J. Christopher Crocker, eds.
1977   The Social Use of Metaphor: Essays on the Anthropology
              of Rhetoric. Philadelphia: University of Pennsylvania
              Press.

Schechtman, Joseph B.
1963   The Refugee in the World: Displacement and Integration. New York: A. S. Barnes.

Shakabpa, Tsepon W. D.
1967   Tibet: A Political History. New Haven, Conn.: Yale University Press.

Shes-Bya
1977   "Statement" (*gsal-bsgrags*). April, pp. 19–22.

Shibles, Warren, ed.
1972   Essays on Metaphor. Whitewater, Wis.: Language Press.

Snellgrove, David, and Hugh E. Richardson
1968   A Cultural History of Tibet. New York: Praeger.

Stein, Rolf A.
1972   Tibetan Civilization. Trans. by John Driver. Stanford, Calif.: Stanford University Press. (French original 1962)

Schwartz, Marc J.; Victor Turner; and Arthur Tuden
1966   Political Anthropology. Chicago: Aldine.

Tambiah, Stanley J.
1977   World Conqueror and World Renouncer: A Study of Buddhism and Polity in Thailand against a Historical Background. Cambridge: Cambridge University Press.

Tenzing Chhodak
1981   "Education of Tibetan Refugees: Characteristics and Conditions of Learning Environments in Selected Tibetan Schools in India." Ph.D. dissertation, Center for International Education, University of Massachusetts, Amherst.

Tibet and the Chinese People's Republic: A Report to the International Commission of Jurists by Its Legal Inquiry Committee on Tibet
1960   Geneva: International Commission of Jurists.

Tibet under Chinese Communist Rule: A Compilation of Refugee Statements 1958–1975
1976   Dharamsala: Information and Publicity Office of H. H. the Dalai Lama.

Tibetan Review
1968a   "Statement of His Holiness the Dalai Lama on the Occasion of the Ninth Anniversary of the Lhasa Uprising on the 10th March, 1959." March, pp. 8–9.
1968b   "The Tibetan Schools Society: The Story of the

Education of Tibetan Refugee Children in India."
September, pp. 8–11.

1969a   "A Decade in Exile." April, pp. 4–5.

1969b   "The Lhasa Uprising and Aftermath." March, p. 2.

1970   "Text of the Address by H. H. the Dalai Lama on the Closing Day of the First Tibetan Youth Conference, Dharamsala, October 14, 1970." November, pp. 6–8.

1972a   "Dharma Course in Dharamsala." December, p. 8.

1972b   "Tibetan Freedom Conference." August, pp. 4–5.

1973a   "A Link between Past and Present." January-February, pp. 9–10.

1973b   "Rulers of Tibet during 2100 Years." March, pp. 10–11.

1973c   "Second Phase in Tibetan Education." January-February, pp. 3, 11.

1973d   "The Tearful Tales of TIRS." July, pp. 7, 13.

1973e   "Tibet in a Decade of Detente." April, p. 3.

1973f   "TIRS: Not a Success Story." July, p. 3.

1974   "What Is Tibet's Cause?" March, p. 6.

1975   "Buddhism: Conclusion Reached by Reasoning." November, pp. 14, 10.

1976a   "Aesthetics and Politics of a Drama." January-February, pp. 11–12.

1976b   "Armed Struggle in the Offing." January-February, pp. 3–4, 7.

1976c   "Dalai Lama Assails Tibetan Complacency." March, pp. 4–5.

1976d   "Higher Tibetan Institute—A Failure?" September, pp. 7–8.

1976e   "The Last Dalai Lama?" March, pp. 3–4.

1976f   "Letters: Editor and Sectarian Harmony." December, pp. 23–24.

1976g   "Letters: Ideal Leadership of Dalai Lama and Lama Teachers." October, pp. 36, 32–35.

1976h   "Letters: Stone Building Is No School." June–July, pp. 20–25.

1976i   "Modern Education for Monks?" December, p. 7.

1976j   "More on Tibetan Schools Education." June–July, pp. 3–4, 19.

1976k   "Peking Sends Chinese Immigrants to Tibet." June–July, pp. 5–8.

1976l   "Situation and Needs of Tibetans in Exile." December, pp. 9–11, 18.

1976m   "The State of Tibetan School Education." April, pp. 3–4.

1976n   "Tibetan Buddhism under American Orientation." January, pp. 7–9.

1977a   "Dalai Lama's Thoughts." August, pp. 22–23.
1977b   "The Morning after the Night Before." July, pp. 3–4.
1977c   "1976 Report of CTSA." May, pp. 6–7, 15.
1977d   "Tibetan Freedom Movement in Delhi."
               February–March, pp. 12–14.
1977e   "Tibetan Settlements in Bylakuppe, South India."
               February–March, pp. 12–14.
1977f   "Varanasi Institute to Come Under CTSA." November,
               p. 10.
1978a   "China's Nuclear Device in Tibet." May, pp. 19–20.
1978b   "Election System to Remain Unchanged." September,
               p.7.
1978c   "Population Figures: Genocide Proved?" July, p. 4.
1978d   "Youths Want Election System Changed." April, p. 10.
1978e   "Youths Will Not Boycott Election." October, p. 7.
1979   "List of Tibetan Buddhist Centres." January, pp. 22–23.
1980a   "China Building Missile Base in Central Tibet."
               February–March, pp. 21–22.
1980b   "The Hammer, Sickle and Pen: Manifesto of the Tibetan
               Communist Party." July, pp. 7–8.
1980c   "10th March Commemoration in the West." April,
               pp. 8–9.
1980d   "Youth Organisation Against Sending Delegations to
               Tibet." July, p. 5.
1982a   "Experiments in Democracy." August, pp. 3, 22.
1982b   "Tibetan Communist Party Is Dissolved."
               February–March, p. 5.
1982c   "Tibetan Parliament Gets a Face Life." August, p. 4.

Tibetan Students Fraternity
1977   Newsletter. Vol. 5, May–October.

Tibetans in Exile: 1959–1969
1969   Dharamsala: Bureau of H. H. the Dalai Lama.

Thubten Jigme Norbu (with Colin M. Turnbull)
1970   Tibet. New York: Simon & Schuster.

Tsering Wangyal
1976   "The Long Road to Utopia." Tibetan Review, December,
               pp. 3–4, 8.

Tucci, Giuseppe
1970   "Die Religionen Tibets. Pp. 5–291 in Die Religionen
               Tibets und der Mongolei by Guiseppe Tucci and Walther
               Heissig. Stuttgart: Kohlhammer.

Turner, Victor
1967   "Betwixt and Between: The Liminal Period in *Rites de
            Passage*." Pp. 93–111 in The Forest of Symbols: Aspects
            of Ndembu Ritual. Ithaca, N.Y.: Cornell University Press.
1969a   "Introduction." Pp. 3–25 in Forms of Symbolic Action.
            Proceedings of the 1969 Annual Spring Meeting of the
            American Ethnological Society, edited by Robert F.
            Spencer. Seattle: University of Washington Press.
1969b   The Ritual Process: Structure and Anti-Structure.
            Chicago: Aldine.
1974   Dramas, Fields, and Metaphors: Symbolic Action in
            Human Society. Ithaca, N.Y.: Cornell University Press.
1975   "Symbolic Studies." Pp. 3–25 in Annual Review of
            Anthropology, edited by Bernard J. Siegel. Stanford,
            Calif.: Stanford University Press.

Vostrikov, Andrei Ivanovich
1962   Tibetskaya istoricheskaya literatura. Moscow: Akademia
            Nauk.

Wallace, Anthony
1961   "Schools in Revolutionary and Conservative Societies."
            Pp. 25–54 in Anthropology and Education, edited by
            Frederick C. Gruber. Philadelphia: University of
            Pennsylvania Press.

Wangyal, D.
1976   "Poisonous View." Tibetan Review, October, p. 32.

Wylie, Turrell V.
1959   "A Standard System of Tibetan Transcription." Harvard
            Journal of Asian Studies, 22:261–276.

Yeshi Dhonden
1976   "What Is Tibetan Medicine?" Trans. by Gyatsho Tsering.
            Pp. 5–11 in An Introduction to Tibetan Medicine, edited
            by Dawa Norbu. Delhi: Tibetan Review.

Index

agricultural settlements, 57,
122–124, 125, 143, 153
ahimsa (non-violence), 127, 133,
138, 157
alienation
of the fieldworker, 2–3, 158, 161
of Tibetans, 2, 151, 155, 157, 174.
See also distanciation
All-India Higher Secondary Examination, 38, 67, 86, 107, 108
ambiguity
of the anthropological situation,
7–8, 7n, 159
of the Dalai Lama, 27, 30, 129,
136, 156, 164, 169
interpretation of, 166–171
of liminal states, 4, 45–46, 165
of the Tibetan situation, 165–166
Amdo (northeastern Tibet), 9n, 14,
20, 66, 140, 177, 178
Andrugtsang, Gompo Tashi, 20
Assembly of Tibetan People's Deputies. *See* Commission of Tibetan People's Deputies
Avalokiteshvara (*spyan-ras-gzigs*)
Dalai Lama as, 25, 27, 30, 95, 129
Tibet's patron bodhisattva, 91, 92

Bacot, J., 91
Balandier, Georges, 27, 44, 129
Barth, Fredrik, 44
Bharati, Agehananda, 74n
Black, Max, 162
bodhisattva, 25, 26, 91, 92, 95, 133,
136
Bonpo Tibetans, 177–178
Boon, James A., 48
Buddhism
associated with Tibetanness,
86–88, 90–92, 99

re-examination of, by Tibetan
youth, 110–113, 130, 131–136,
139
Western interest in, 42, 65, 96,
113, 113n, 125, 130, 136, 142
Buddhist School of Dialectics, 36,
61, 110, 112–113, 125
Buddhist sects, 13, 64, 141, 177
Burke, Kenneth, 44

"cause of Tibet," 89, 108, 139, 145,
150, 151, 154, 162, 163, 164
Central Committee on the Educa-
tion of Tibetan Refugees. *See*
Central Tibetan Schools
Administration
Central Institute of Higher Tibetan
Studies, 58n, 110–112, 125,
131–133. *See also* Tibetan
Language Teachers Training
Program
Central Tibet (*bod*), 86n, 88, 178.
See also Dbus-gtsang
Central Tibetan Schools Administration, 56–59, 61, 108, 111,
119
chos-srid zung-'brel. See "religion
and politics combined"
Cohen, Abner, 44
colonialism, 10, 21, 43, 60
Commission of Tibetan People's
Deputies, 141, 143, 145, 149,
153, 177–179
communism, 21, 130, 132, 132n,
142
"compassion" (*snying-rje*), 53, 92,
100, 102, 105, 133, 137–138,
139, 142, 164
Constitution of Tibet, 29, 140, 141
continuity, cultural, 25, 47, 53, 55,